ReNEW

Traveling the Forgotten Path

J. David Jackson

Screven and Allen Publishing
Marlborough, Massachusetts

What Others Are Saying

"Thoughtfully and thoroughly, David Jackson provides an outstanding do-it-yourself guidebook for pastors and church leadership teams who believe the most effective days of the church they lead are still in the future. Gleaning wisdom from his years as a church leader and consultant, Jackson skillfully demonstrates how insights from the church planting world can be used to spark a fresh season of missional progress for any church that has become discontent with their status quo."

Steve Pike
Founder, Church Multiplication Network
President, Urban Islands Project

"David's insights in ReNEW will help any pastor. With a powerful mix of spiritual encouragement and leadership strategy, this book will be a go-to resource for you. Read it. Learn from it. Lead with it."

Dr. Philip Nation
author of Habits for Our Holiness
and Transformational Discipleship

"I've known David Jackson for more years than either of us would probably like to admit. In all of that time I have always found him to be a gifted mission strategist with a passion to help the local church. With this book David lays out what is at the heart of true revitalization: remembering why the church was planted in the first place and returning to those very things they did at first. I commend this book to any church seeking to glorify God by reaching their community and making disciples."

Mark Clifton
Senior Director of RePlanting
North American Mission Board, SBC

#renewbook

"Every once in a while you come across a book that makes so much sense, that you stop and think, 'Why hadn't I thought of this before?' David Jackson has just written that book. From one who has both personally started new churches and who has coached scores more into existence, David gives a practical application of Revelation 2:5 to stalled, stuck, and troubled churches from a unique perspective that could only come from his experience. Pastors, replanters, and revitalizing leaders alike will find great wisdom, inspiration, and instruction in these pages. "

Jeff Christopherson
VP Send Network, North American Mission Board, SBC
author of Kingdom First: Starting Churches that Shape Movements, *and*
Kingdom Matrix: Designing Churches for the Kingdom of God

"ReNEW understands and gives a clear path for those interested in church planting and church health. David has the wisdom, experience, and knowledge to speak to these much needed topics. He gives us a way to evaluate where we are, dream about where we want to go, and steps to follow to help us get there. I recommend this book to everyone interested in the church being what God intended it to be!"

Larry Barker
Director of Church Planting
BMAA Missions
larryjbarker.com

"David Jackson leads in one of the must unreached people group's in our nation-New England. Through his years of ministry, he's learned to ask hard questions, seek practical solutions, and nurture church growth. In this book, he shares his hard won lessons—the kind that church leaders everywhere will be encouraged and challenged by."

Margaret Feinberg
author of Flourish

"Stop wasting your time with quick fix books about revitalizing a church and grab a hold of *ReNEW: Traveling the Forgotten Path* by David Jackson. I have known Dr. Jackson for more than thirty years and I know that you will not be disappointed with the nuggets you draw from this work. Wrapped around a journey motif you will discover items to equip pastors and planters for this effort. David speaks from a wealth of experience and has been an accomplished church practitioner for more than thirty years. Read him, learn from him, and tell others about him. You can't go wrong with this veteran church leader and coach! Get started and watch the Lord 'ReNew' your church and return it to the forgotten path."

Tom Cheyney
Founder & Directional Leader
The Renovate National Church Revitalization Conference
Executive Editor of The Church Revitalizer Magazine
author of Slaying the Dragons of Church Revitalization and Renewal

"Renewal leadership requires wisdom, intentionality, and grit. David's book informs and empowers these church replanters with key lessons hammered out in the church planting realm and how to apply them to the world of revitalization and/or replanting. *ReNEW* needs to be on the reading list of anyone serious about leading renewal efforts in their church."

Dr. Jim Harrell
President and Founder of Overseed
author of Church Replanter

"ReNEW is a fresh look at an old subject from a leader with decades of experience and priceless wisdom. If taken seriously and applied relentlessly, this tool could give your church a ReNew-ed future."

Gary Rohrmayer
Church Multiplication Partners
www.multiplychurches.org

"Established churches need church plants just as much as church plants need established churches. Just imagine the impact if both learned from each other, and worked together to reach their community and region for Christ! Journey along with David, as he maps out a way forward for Kingdom impact and collaboration."

Daniel Im
author of No Silver Bullets
coauthor of Planting Missional Churches
Director of Church Multiplication at NewChurches.com
and teaching pastor

ReNEW

Traveling the Forgotten Path

J. David Jackson

#renewbook

Copyright © 2017 by J. David Jackson

ISBN-13: 978-0692998205 (Screven and Allen Publishing)
ISBN-10: 0692998209

All rights reserved. Printed in the United States of America. No part of this book may be used or reproduced in any manner whatsoever without written permission except in the case of brief quotations embodied in critical articles and reviews.

Printed in the United States of America

Unless otherwise noted, all Scripture quotations are taken from the Christian Standard Bible, copyright © 2017, by Holman Bible Publishers. Used by permission. Christian Standard Bible, CSB are federally registered trademarks of Christian Bible Publishers.

Cover photo: Chad Madden, unSplash.com

PREVIOUS WORKS BY THE AUTHOR

PlantLIFE: Principles and Practices in Church Planting (2008)

PLANTED: Starting Well, Growing Strong (2012)

"Remember then how far you have fallen; repent, and **do the works you did at first**. Otherwise, I will come to you and remove your lampstand from its place, unless you repent."

Revelation 2:5

#renewbook

DEDICATION

To my parents,

Jimmy and Cleo Jackson

who
invested their life and love in me,
introduced me to Jesus and to Joyce, and
showed me what it means to serve others, for Jesus' sake

~ xiv ~

#renewbook

ACKNOWLEDGEMENTS

A book like this doesn't happen without the help and encouragement of many others. This is certainly the case here. My thanks go out to many people, none more than my wife, Joyce, who has been my constant support and primary cheerleader through the entire process. She has assisted me in numerous other ways. Suffice it to say, if this book is helpful and beneficial to you and your ministry, I suspect it is the result of her involvement in improving the content and shaping the presentation. She does all of this with such love and grace, and for that I stand amazed.

Several individuals have served as readers in the process to help me edit the material, and to provide suggestions to make the book better and more applicable to "the real world" of revitalization. I'd like to thank them for their efforts on my behalf, as well. Joel Thrasher, Ron Blankenship, Ken Cavey, Shannon Baker, and Chris Adams have all contributed ideas and encouragement to me that have helped improve what you read here.

I would like to thank the churches where I have served, who experienced many of these principles and ideas put into practice. These include Faith Baptist Church in Glen Burnie; Maryland, Gethsemane Baptist Church in Glenwood, Maryland; First Southern Baptist Church in Monterey Park, California; and Maine Street Baptist Church in Brunswick, Maine. Where I have made mistakes, you have offered me grace; where the hard work has succeeded, we have celebrated our teamwork together. I am better and wiser because of you. My prayer is that the churches where we ministered are healthier, stronger, more discerning, and more evangelistic, as a result of our service.

I also express my gratitude to the organizations I've worked with who enabled me to put pen to paper and share these learnings with you, the reader. To the Baptist Convention of Maryland/Delaware, I am thankful for the sabbatical time to draft the early research and writing of this material. To the *Turning Around Journey* cohort, and to colleague Randy Millwood, I express thanks for the opportunity to learn together as we journeyed through our revitalization experiences for a year. To the Baptist Convention of New England and the North American Mission Board, I am grateful for the support in completing the work. To my publisher, Screven and Allen, thanks for the assistance in getting the book into its final form. My prayer is that the content here will be useful in the efforts of churches within our region, and beyond, for God's glory.

    Finally, I am most profoundly thankful to God, for the opportunity to serve Him and to write out these lessons in ways that may assist others in dealing with the difficult challenge of revitalization. He is always able to do *"exceedingly abundantly beyond all we ask or imagine"* (Ephesians 3:20). My hope and prayer is that this book will be a catalyst to dream big dreams for the future, and even more, to follow our big God more closely in extending His kingdom through the generations yet to come.

J. David Jackson, January 2018

TABLE OF CONTENTS

Foreword by Ed Stetzer
xxi

Introduction
1

PART ONE...
REMEMBER THE FORMER THINGS

1: EXTERNAL ELEMENTS
The Exercise Every Church Needs – Apply to Your Setting – Questions to Consider – Digging Deeper
11

2: FOUNDATIONAL FACTORS
The Foundation Every Church Requires – Apply to Your Setting – Questions to Consider – Digging Deeper
27

PART TWO...
I AM DOING A NEW THING

3: PREPARING FOR THE JOURNEY
"This is the Winter of Our Discontent" – A Coalition of the Willing – Two Other Issues that Must Be Addressed – Apply to Your Setting – Questions to Consider – Digging Deeper
41

4: MAPPING THE ADVENTURE
Your GPS – Growing Up – What Goes Up Must Come Down? – The Importance of Vision – Apply to Your Setting – Questions to Consider – Digging Deeper
59

5: DEALING WITH BAGGAGE
Packing for the Trip – "Unmentionables" – Image is Everything? – Constraining Structure – Apply to Your Setting – Questions to Consider – Digging Deeper

73

6: TOUR GUIDE
Know Yourself – Longevity has its Benefits – Rallying the Troops – Empowering Others – Apply to Your Setting – Questions to Consider – Digging Deeper

91

7: RESOURCING THE JOURNEY
It All Starts with the Heart – Status Quo=Disobedience – Job One – Simple is a Plus – Programming is Not a Bad Word – Staffing for Growth – Apply to Your Setting – Questions to Consider – Digging Deeper

103

8: ENCOUNTERING THE UNEXPECTED
Getting to Know the Natives – Relationships are Messy – Difficult People – Get Outside the Walls - Meet and Greet – Serve with a Smile – Getting the People Involved – Apply to Your Setting – Questions to Consider – Digging Deeper

119

9: COLLECTING SOUVENIRS
Generosity – Making More Disciples – Leadership Development – For the Sake of the Kingdom – Legacy Planting – Moments in Time – Exceedingly Abundantly Beyond… – Apply to Your Setting – Questions to Consider – Digging Deeper

139

10: ARRIVING AT YOUR DESTINATION
Adaptability and Creativity – Celebration – Recalibration – Apply to Your Setting – Questions to Consider – Digging Deeper

153

11: CANCELING THE TRIP
"We Didn't Really Want This" – "This is Too Costly" – "It's Too Hard" – "What about Us?" – "We Don't Really Care that Much" – Apply to Your Setting – Questions to Consider – Digging Deeper

165

Epilogue
177

Notes
181

About the Author
189

~ XX ~

FOREWORD
by Ed Stetzer

I remember when I was planting my first church in Buffalo, NY. Donna (my wife) was a substitute teacher and I painted houses on the side as we got through by sheer force and grit. Back then, there was no such thing as church planting networks or denominational support; it was a minefield where most planters failed. And we came close more times than I can remember.

But what came out of that experience was something beautiful: a unique expression of God's Kingdom. Neighbors were being reached, people came to faith, more churches were planted and, like many plants, there was a vibrancy and energy that seems strangely absent in established churches. And it is this absence that incites a question: what would happen if established churches could ignite that spark of vibrancy and Gospel movement that comes with a church plant, while still retaining the benefits of permanency and maturity?

And that is where *ReNEW: Traveling the Forgotten Path* gives us both wisdom and encouragement to rediscover what has made the Church thrive for two millennia. This book is not about going back to old methodologies or the 'good ol' days', but rather to "do the works you did at first" (Rev. 2:5), 'works' like reaching the unreached for Jesus, serving our neighbors, and not relying on facilities, programs, and organizational structures to advance the organic, living, active Church into the world.

ReNEW clarifies what makes church plants effective and translates these principles for the established pastor. Part of what makes new churches effective for the Gospel is how they reach and retain those who are far from Jesus. Beginning any new venture inspires those involved to contribute towards its growth, and Christians do this through evangelism and service. It's an external focus that is necessitated by survival, and also a genuine passion to see people come to know and follow Jesus. Additionally, church plants draw entrepreneurial leadership towards the newness, and this pushes an already creative endeavor even further into creatively exploring how to reach new people groups and demographics. Everything is new, in 'beta,' and the Gospel advances because of it.

This book addresses and clarifies what makes church plants effective, and then helps established church pastors to translate those principles into developed church systems. Specific principles that incubate an environment of innovation can be translated to generate excitement and momentum towards established churches. It shows that pastors who recruit well and often into the vision can bring about a critical mass of buy-in for Gospel change in their context. This book shows us that the same zeal in a church plant is possible in established churches.

ReNEW reminds us that the focus of the church isn't a destination, it's a journey that leads us to Jesus. God has a mission since the Fall to bring the world back to Himself, and in the culmination of that mission He sent His Son to be the one who draws the world back to Himself. In fact, He gave us Himself in the Person and Work of Jesus so that we might know Him and become like Him.

He has given us His Church as the primary agent of blessing in the world, commissioned and called to see His glory extend throughout the world and Jesus' fame proclaimed to the nations. He has not called this community of faith to static complacency, but towards movement and progression with responsibility that extends to every follower of Jesus. And this movement outwards requires bold, trailblazing leadership that unites and emboldens the church to new levels of ministry and mission for the fame of Jesus.

In order to see this type of leadership emerge in established churches, pastors must become trailblazers, going out in front and drawing their congregations to come with him. Entropy is the natural state of human beings, and we will always tend towards passivity and regression rather than advancement and progression. We need strong pastors with a passion for the lost and the boldness to set aside any encumbrances to seeing people come to Jesus as the primary function of the church. This book helps equip pastors from the lull of the ordinary and familiar, into the unknown and the extraordinary. How churches respond to this visionary leadership not only determines its future, but the future of those it hopes to reach.

This book helps equip pastors from the lull of the ordinary and familiar, into the unknown and the extraordinary.

-Dr. Ed Stetzer holds the Billy Graham Distinguished Chair at Wheaton College

~ xxiv ~

ReNEW:
Traveling the Forgotten Path

INTRODUCTION

Pastor Stephen breathed a sigh of relief. The past three years had been filled with struggle and anxiety. Some of the concerns in his church had been obvious and early on he had done what he could to address them. Others failed to surface until much later. Surprisingly, he came to realize that some of these concerns were organic; some were organizational. Other concerns were sociological, while still others were relational in nature.

Pastor Stephen recently met Joe,[1] the new church planter in town, at Joe's initial community ministerial council meeting. At that meeting Joe announced that he had come here to plant a new church, because of the large number of unreached people in this town. Pastor Stephen's reaction was initially very predictable. He wasn't excited to know of Joe's presence in this location, since he had been here for almost seven years already. In some ways, he felt threatened by his presence; after all, Joe was from the same denominational tribe as Pastor Stephen. And he wasn't so sure he approved of all the methods Joe was using in his new church. He worried the Gospel was being compromised, that people would leave his church for "greener pastures," and that honestly, his self-esteem as a minister, having labored hard with little to show for it, would take a hit and not recover.

"Why can't we grow like we should? What's keeping us from experiencing the blessing of God, like Joe's new church? What will it take for us to find the keys that unlock a powerful future for First Church?" Pastor Stephen found himself asking these questions virtually every day as he wrestled with the issues of his church. He prayed that God would reveal

#renewbook

something—anything—that would renew the church, giving it hope and purpose once again.

    I travel. A lot. My work takes me all over North America. A significant portion of my travel equips me to lead our church planting ministry more effectively. I learn new ideas and concepts, network with other continental leaders, and experience ministry life as it is lived in other places. In the process, my mind races ahead as I begin to connect new, innovative strategies to the church planting systems we currently have in place. We never take for granted our success; rather, we realize that becoming too comfortable with the way things are will tempt us into complacency. It will deceive us into thinking we can stay the same, yet still reach people effectively.

    Church planters are by nature innovators. They are constantly living on the cutting edge, thinking of ways to reach people in their community more effectively. It is not hard to convince a genuine church planter of the value found in such thinking. They have a built-in, God-given desire to live "outside the box," and as a result, they will lead their new church to do so. Sometimes, the idea they attempt fails; often though, it succeeds. In both situations, they make progress that enables the new congregation to be more effective in living out its mission for Jesus.

    A large majority of churches in North America are not this way. Even more in Europe fit this description. For more than three decades now, the American church has noted the decline not only in church participation, but even in the attitudes and values held by people in regards to church life. While the public at large has not necessarily "written off" Jesus, an overwhelming majority have done so with the church. They no longer feel church is relevant, helpful, or practical to the world in which they live.[2]

    Established churches—defined here somewhat arbitrarily as those over fifteen years of age—struggle with this reality far more than younger churches do. There are many reasons for this. Regardless of the reasons, however, the established church in many places is vulnerable and finds itself in a precarious position today. This is not to suggest that the established church fails to be resilient in the face of great obstacles; in fact, it is often very difficult to end. However, a wide majority of established churches in the Western world have "plateaued" or are in decline, both in size and influence. Many are asking if there is a way to reverse this trend.

WHAT CAN NEW CHURCHES TEACH US?

Years ago, as a young, newly married adult I thought when children came along I would do the teaching, and they would do the learning. Was I ever mistaken! Sure, our three children have learned many lessons about life from my wife Joyce and me. But they have also taught me so many things about life, the world, and even myself that I did not expect or anticipate. I would have failed to embrace so many possibilities and opportunities, if I had been unwilling to learn from them, regardless of their age or experience. God reminds us in His Word, *"From the mouths of infants and nursing babies, you have established a stronghold on account of your adversaries in order to silence the enemy and the avenger"* (Psalm 8:2). In other words, in God's economy even the youngest and most innocent have ways to humble the strongest and most educated.

We see this all the time in the word of technology. The young men and women who grew up with laptops and smartphones from birth have the ability to "reverse mentor" those of us who are more averse to the trappings of a full frontal assault by the technological world. We can all learn, if we are willing.

In the same way, established churches can learn a great deal from new churches, if they will simply try. Now at first blush, church plants and established churches may not seem to have a lot in common. Established churches typically have a facility; church plants do not. Established churches have money in the bank (not necessarily a lot); church plants live month to month in most settings. Established churches have programs with regular routines and processes for their existence; church plants have not created these yet. There are many other differences, as well, which will be explored in this book. So, how can they teach established, storied, and significant churches?

Here's how. All churches—regardless of age—have one crucial thing in common: they all started at some point. In other words, established churches were once a church plant themselves. They once grappled with the same issues church plants grapple with today. In fact, research indicates that these early years in the life of established churches were usually among the very best years of growth experienced, no matter how old the church is now.3

> **What if an established church could renew the experience of its first few years as a congregation, but with the wisdom and experience of many years in ministry?**

What if an established church could renew the experience of its first few years as a congregation, but with the wisdom and experience of many years in ministry? What if it began again to act like a church plant in its thinking and behavior, yet with all the benefits and advantages of a church of many years? What if these mature churches dared to recover the keys to their early success and incorporate them into their current community life? This book is written to address this possibility.

Let me be clear: I'm not suggesting the established church give in to the vocal cry to return to the "good ol' days." These days, typically defined as the optimal years of growth and success in the church's life, produced time-dated strategies that worked in a world that has long since disappeared, where church was valued by society and there were extremely limited options for community activity, especially on Sunday morning. Rather, I'm talking about traveling back even further, to recover the principles and practices of the church in its earliest days, to *"do the works you did at first"* (Revelation 2:5), and to reclaim its first love. This correction focuses the church back on relationships (with God and others) and evangelism, its inherent strengths, and not on programming and facilities.

#renewbook

Recently, I traveled back to the city where I received my first master's degree. I wandered onto the campus and spent hours just looking around; my, how it had changed! New buildings were evident everywhere, and the community around the school had aged. It was a different place than I knew some thirty years ago. Even the students looked so much younger than I remembered: could I have ever looked that young?! I found a hallway occupied by photographs of many of my former professors, and as a result, found myself reminiscing about many of the wonderful lessons and experiences I had shared with them. It was as if the floodgates had been opened, and memory after memory came rushing in. It helped me recapture some of my past, some of what has made me the person I am today.

Established churches need to recapture part of their past. Some will argue, "You can't go home again." I agree. To be sure, it is impossible to reconstruct the countless variables involved in the beginning of a new church. These include the environment at that time, the location for meeting, the lack of church history, and the planter, as well. These things, in reality, can't be relived. However, the principles and processes applied in those days can be remembered, re-learned, and implemented again. Moreover, they can be implemented with the advantages of wisdom, resources, and experience, which offer the potential for even greater growth and impact.

WHAT YOU WILL FIND IN THIS BOOK

To do this, my goal is to help you understand and apply several realities. First, this book will review the characteristics that enable a new church to grow so effectively in the early years of its existence. These elements are fleshed out in greater detail in my previous book, *PLANTED: Starting Well, Growing Strong* (Screven and Allen Publishing, 2012).[4] Here, we will simply overview the highlights of these ten characteristics and suggest ways in which established churches can implement these elements.

Second, this book will examine the life of an established church. We will help the reader identify where the church is located in its own lifecycle and determine if it is "acting its age." We will identify obstacles in the aging process that block its continued growth and suggest ways for overcoming these obstacles. These obstacles include heart issues, as well as sociological issues.

This book is more linear than its predecessor. In other words, the first section of the book lays the foundation for what comes in the latter half of the book. Because of this, it needs to be read first, rather than moving about randomly. The material in the second section, however, can be addressed in any order, as the need or concern arises or interests the reader.

At the end of each chapter, *Apply in Your Setting, Coaching Questions,* and *Digging Deeper* will recommend some additional activity the reader can do to process the material even further. These are best used in a group or team setting, but may be of profit to individual readers, as well. This section will also suggest other resources that may be of help to the reader, if interested. My attempt here is to encourage you to apply the information in this book in ways that will assist you and your church leadership in seeing the church grow again, even as it did in its earliest years.

As I mentioned at the beginning of this introduction, I travel a lot. The goal of these journeys is typically to get me from where I am currently located to where I need to be. This book seeks to help you do just that. It is a vehicle to transport you to the destination your church needs. Over the years I have learned, though, that there is also much that can be learned on the trip itself. While the journey is not always enjoyable, it is always beneficial. So, do not miss the lessons of God along the way! These lessons are often the most meaningful, and potentially, the most long-reaching in impact and significance for both you and your church.

So, if you are reading this book, I am going to make the assumption you are interested in seeing your church grow, and you are willing to entertain the possibility that to renew it may mean to rediscover some of the wisdom of your predecessors in that congregation. If this is true of you, then I salute you: you are a courageous leader! You are willing to confront the shadows of the past, the demons of the present, and the unknowns of the future, with the lessons God has shared.

    No longer do these lessons have to be forgotten. They can be recovered and renewed in the life of the church.

~ 8 ~

PART ONE

"Remember the Former Things…"

~ 10 ~

EXTERNAL ELEMENTS

Pastor Stephen was amazed. Joe, the new church planter in town, had only been here for a year and his fledgling congregation already had over a hundred people involved. "How did he do that?" Pastor Stephen wondered. "I've been here for more than six years and we haven't been able to reach half that many."

He watched Joe from a distance and noted that the new church was intentionally active in the community. Since they didn't have their own facility with weeklong access, they spent considerable time intersecting the lives of community residents. "They are always doing something different," Stephen thought, as he recollected the immigration and naturalization classes they taught, the Little League team they sponsored, the city park for which they cared, the school they had adopted, and the local government task force they had joined.

They had a heart for those without Jesus; this was evident to Pastor Stephen. They were always present and serving wherever unchurched people could be found: the recreation fields, the local bars, the community center nearby, the pool hall down the street. They were finding ways to minister to these people, from coaching their soccer teams, to serving as designated drivers to get them home safely at night, to teaching computer and swimming classes. They parlayed these experiences into relationships with the people they were meeting, inviting them to their homes for dinner and introducing them to other friends. As a result, many of these formerly unchurched individuals and families were becoming followers of Christ.

Redemption Fellowship—the name of church planter Joe's new church—was building alliances in town, too, with others who wanted to see Christ make a difference there. The local Covenant church and the Assembly church had joined with them in providing food for those displaced by the awful tornado last year. They had also worked with the local Red Cross on their own disaster relief efforts. In addition, Pastor Stephen became aware of the fact that Joe was meeting with the other church planters in the area, likely for mutual support and learning.

Pastor Stephen reflected on the experiences of First Church. They were certainly very different from those of Joe. He wondered if such experiences could ever be his own.

In the past fifty years, Americans have suffered an obesity problem. In fact, it has reached such epidemic proportions that several efforts are being made to reverse this dangerous trend. Nutrition guidelines are now the norm in most restaurants. Exercise has been encouraged, with Hollywood celebrities throwing their support behind the efforts. Even the former First Lady of the United States made a visible, concerted effort to motivate children to embrace a lifestyle to keep them healthy and strong.[5]

While there may be many variables at work in the lives of every individual that contribute to this concern, all experts agree that two factors are absolutely essential to overcoming the trend toward obesity: good nutrition and physical exercise. Without these positive influencers, the human body will become unhealthy and in danger of disease. These negative consequences cover the spectrum of impact on a person's well-being, from sluggish thinking and muscular atrophy to chronic conditions, like diabetes and heart disease.

The church has an obesity problem, too. During the same period of history, churches have become obsessed with slick programming, amazing presentations, and information overload. They have fed on these things so much, they have seemingly become addicted to the "oohs" and "aahs" of cool novelties and forgotten the reason for feeding on the Word of God in the first place.

The Word of God nourishes us for living out our faith. It provides the fuel for our service. It prepares and energizes us for our own ministry in the world. It strengthens our "spiritual immune system" and keeps us healthy from the temptations and "diseases" Satan tries to send our way. It is to be lived out in active service for Christ.

Three decades ago, contemporary Christian artists sang about this dilemma affecting the church. Keith Green reminded his listeners that God commanded, "To obey is better than sacrifice," (1 Samuel 15:22) challenging Christ-followers to more than just church attendance.[6] Amy Grant sang about the "Fat Baby" syndrome in church life, those who want to feed more and more on the Word of God, but never exercise its message outside the walls of the church building.[7]

Today it is time for churches to acknowledge they cannot be healthy followers of Christ, if they fail to get outside the walls of their meeting place and exercise their faith.

Today churches must acknowledge they cannot be healthy followers of Christ, if they fail to get outside the walls of their meeting place and exercise their faith. An indoor experience alone leaves a church weak, unhealthy, and in danger of disease. Churches must get out of their doors and into the mission field.

Church plants understand this; their station in life demands they be outdoors a lot. They have no facility of their own (this is true, at least for the wide majority of them, until several years into their life). They have a great deal of energy. The passion of their life together and the newness of their experience excites them. The exuberance of their joy and the vitality of their hope fuel them toward others. They are hungry to be meaningful in their community and to connect with the people who live where they live. All of this translates into a scattered church, more than even a gathered church.

THE EXERCISE EVERY CHURCH NEEDS

In *PLANTED: Starting Well, Growing Strong*, five key characteristics were unpacked that reveal why church plants are so effective in their earliest years. These external characteristics demonstrate the essential nature of an every-day walk with the LORD and the impact it makes on others around them. Such visible activity is evidence of a heart devoted to God's love for all people; it lives out the belief that "we are blessed to be a blessing." So what are these characteristics?

First, there is the power of relationships.[8] New churches find their primary value and strength in relationships. They focus on building community among the attendees. In fact, they recognize that just because people come to a worship experience doesn't mean they are connected or even share anything in common with the Body of Christ...yet. They seek for newcomers to experience the "common unity" that becomes "community" in the new church's life.

Relationships: Effective churches ALWAYS value people more than programs.

How do they do this? They show it in the way they live out their existence. Effective new churches ALWAYS value people more than programs. In many ways, this is easy to do. Church plants usually don't have facilities to value. Most don't have big budgets or bank accounts to grab their attention. Usually, they don't have large staffs to manage. Moreover, they realize they cannot compete with the programming of the big(ger) church down the street. All they have are relationships, and they must nurture them well.

Relationships depend on interaction, which leads to interdependence, if done well. New churches know that simply touching a life is not enough; they must invest in that life. Consequently, preaching cannot build relationships. Frankly, the worship experience as a whole does little to engender relationships. It is an imperfect, incomplete substitute easily adopted by a majority of churches today.

Small groups or Sunday School classes get closer to the

heart of investment. In fact, they can be a major vehicle for relationship-building. Unfortunately, they are often not used in this way. Rather than relational, community-building experience, these intentional groupings are usually spent on content and information. These are task-oriented. This is not bad, in and of itself, especially if a church has other ways to build relationships. Unfortunately, though, most do not, and they assume incorrectly that in these groups community and relationships are being developed, when they are not.

Investment in relationships requires time together in interactive, give-and-take experiences of life. It goes beyond scheduled classes or meetings and requires informal gatherings of couples and groups, showing hospitality and learning to love one another. Care and concern has to go beyond programming.

In busy churches, with a regular, established routine, it is easy to filter out newcomers or have no margin for the extra time necessary to build relationships. Already-connected people have found what they value and schedule for it accordingly. But newcomers are different. While the preaching or an event/program may have originally interested them in the church, it will be the relationships they develop that keep them coming, week after week.

In many ways, these effective new churches function more like a family...and it shows. They know each other. They accept each other. They support each other. They value each other. They love each other. These are the things people were created to need and experience. Church plants do all they can to enhance the positive familial relationships they foster, and it provides a healthy, nurturing environment in which newcomers can flourish.

When done well, this results in positive word-of-mouth, relational advertising for the church. In fact, nothing is as effective in publicizing a church as its constituents sharing with others the impact their church has made upon them. While marketing methods vary from time-to-time and in measure of their success, nothing has stood the test of time and found the same overwhelming response as a friend sharing with another friend personally. It is genuine, authentic and personal. It is unsolicited and appears to be given without personal gain. It is heartfelt and other-focused. It is sincere and without pretense. There is no wonder why it makes such a powerful impact on others.

Second, new churches are passionate about reaching those apart from Jesus with the Gospel.[9] This often serves as a driving motivation, bringing the church into existence. Planters and those who are a part of their core nucleus want others to experience the love of Christ, so powerful and meaningful in their own lives. They take seriously the co-mission of Christ, to *"Go, therefore, and make disciples of all nations [people groups]..."* (Matthew 28:19).

They do this, motivated by many reasons. For one, they remember that someone else took the time and made the effort to share with them about the grace of God. They recollect the life they had before Christ and the difference He has made in transforming them; they know the power of the Gospel. They count it an honor and a privilege Christ has invited them to join Him in this mission on earth.

Passion for the Lost: Effective churches remain constant; they keep their heart on evangelism.

Perhaps more than anything, they believe that lost people matter to God. They live out their theology, which teaches them, *"Christ also suffered for sins once for all, the righteous for the unrighteous, that He might bring you to God"* (1 Peter 3:18). As a result, they refuse to neglect or ignore lost people. The Gospel compels them to share. It reminds them lost people need to be found. They need to be made aware of God's invitation.

For lost people to know these things, followers of Christ must genuinely care for them. Caring for them requires a heart of unconditional love that sees beyond their reaction and rejection. They meet the hard, resistant heart with patient perseverance and authentic concern. They strive to speak the message of acceptance and forgiveness, accompanied by the example of their lives. Such followers refuse to let others live without knowing the hope that is within them, and how others can come to experience it, too.

#renewbook

In effective new churches, this passion is never forgotten or abandoned. It is not replaced or usurped by other concerns. It remains the driving motivation for the ministry the church plant does, even its reason for being and mission here on earth. This is huge, because it does not take long before other concerns challenge this priority. The worship experience on the weekends demands time, money, and energy. Those already reached cry out for more attention. Expectations of what a church ought to be and do threaten to bring shifts in effort and focus.

Effective new churches remain constant. They keep their heart on evangelism. They "think like a lost person." They plan accordingly. They always advocate for those who are not here…yet.

This impacts how they do ministry. It informs their objectives and strategies. It clarifies the mission. Advocacy gives voice to their theology. It adds vitality to their life together and it embraces urgency. It keeps the main thing, the main thing.

So, new churches that are growing are doing so because they are reaching the lost with the Gospel, not because churched people are transferring their membership. Sure, some other churched people will join them, but they are a rare breed: they are ones who don't come with a consumer attitude (what does the church have to offer me), but rather a servant heart (what do I have to offer the church). They recognize that the only consumers of church should be those as yet without Jesus.

Because this is true, one of the key objectives of these effective new churches is to build bridges that connect to the world of the unreached. To that end, church plants seek to be practical and relevant in the methodology they use. They seek to speak the language of lost people, to act in a way they would understand, and to address the world of their needs.

This is often different from the personal preferences and opinions planters and their new church members hold. If choices were made simply based on their own likes and dislikes, these new churches would do many things differently. However, these churches believe emphatically that they exist,

#renewbook

not for their own benefit, but for the benefit of the world around them that still needs to know Jesus. And this makes all the difference in why they do what they do.

Third, effective new churches realize the people they are called to reach will rarely, if ever, simply show up on their doorstep.[10] No matter how good the worship experience may be, unless the Spirit draws them, lost people will not come and be a part. Rather, these church plants believe that their adherents MUST go to them. They get out of their seats and into the community.

To do so, they must understand that very community where they are located. They must exegete (dissect and analyze) it in many ways: demographically, psychographically, historically, and spiritually, at the very least. In addition, they must understand who they are and how they can best connect and influence the community around them for Christ. This requires the new church not just to know their community, but to love it, as well.

> **Incarnational as well as Attractional: Effective churches must get out of their seats and into the community.**

A great place to start in learning to love your community is to pray for it. When we started our third church plant in Weymouth, Massachusetts, we decided to do two things to inform our heads and our hearts about the people who lived there: we prayerwalked the town, and we prayed through the phonebook.

How did we do this? Monthly, we invited our church family to join together to walk through the town, street by street, and to pray with God-given insight for what we saw and felt. We would divide up as prayer teams, in twos or threes, and after group instructions and prayer, we would journey down assigned streets to pray as God led us. Over the course of 38 months, we prayed our way past 55,000 residents and businesses in our town. Twice the local news took notice of us and wrote articles (both favorable) about our efforts. But more than this, the experience placed an evangelistic burden on our hearts to reach the people in our town, ones who lived there among us, but as yet were not a part of our new church.

We also prayed weekly for the residents of our community. Accessing a directory of residents that was organized by streets, we prayed in smaller group settings for those who lived on certain roads. We did this throughout the several years I served as pastor of Community. Though we knew few of the residents ourselves, it personalized them and kept our focus outward on those who still needed Christ.

Every church can do these things. Walking through your neighborhood or workplace, progressing through a list of names, streets, or addresses, and praying regularly: these are activities even the youngest among us can do that can make a difference. The key is intentionality. Sacrificing time and energy for eternal dividends leads to service opportunities.

Effective church plants then give themselves away through servant evangelism. These "acts of kindness" keep Christ-followers centered on humility and service, key characteristics in Jesus' own ministry. In addition, they enable the new church to demonstrate the love of Christ in practical, relevant ways before the eyes of a lost, unbelieving world. This disarms the critiques lobbied against believers as self-absorbed, judgmental hypocrites, and it replaces them with an experiential image of Christ-followers as authentic, sincere servants who recognize their actions speak louder than words.

These strategies invest in the lives of others eternally through temporal means. They offer the response to time-dated, felt needs as a way for others to see Christ through the lives of His children with no strings attached. More times than not, they plant spiritual seeds rather than harvest fruit. That this is not the ultimate desire or intent is certainly understood, but it is often a necessary prerequisite. The theology of these young churches enables them to trust God to grow the seeds planted in His own time and way. After all, He alone is able to "save" anyone.

This approach additionally gets the Body participating in ministry, out into the community where the unreached people are, and it adds an excitement and vitality to the life of the new church. Attendees can tangibly see the difference they are making. It is a more organic way of involving believers in witness and makes much of the "light and salt" Jesus proclaimed they are to be. For the community at large, servant evangelism builds credibility and integrity, which promotes goodwill and fosters holistic thinking about the presence of the new church and its impact on the town. It develops a winsome reception to their presence and a positive reputation for on-going ministry over the years to come.

Fourth, effective new churches realize they must be creative and innovative.[11] This is not an option or simply personal preference. New churches understand that old forms and methods have appeal to certain people; others will only be reached in new ways and approaches. While established churches have found a routine that typically works well for those already reached, new churches believe that many unreached people would in fact have already responded if such approaches also appealed to them. Simply put, different methods are needed to reach different people.

Good church planters realize this, and as a result, they are constantly asking, "Why do we do what we do?"[12] They determine their course of action based upon the purpose they are attempting to achieve. And since that purpose involves reaching those without Jesus, often they ask them what seekers would look for in a church, if ever interested. Additionally, they find out directly from the unchurched what obstacles are keeping them from considering Christ and His church, at all. As a result, they seek to address their concerns in the way the new congregation "does church."

> **Creative and Innovative: Effective churches are constantly asking, "Why do we do what we do?" and determine their course of action based upon the purpose they are attempting to achieve.**

In decision-making, too, they tend to be *avant-garde*. Unconventional thinkers, including those on the fringe of integrated church life, are given the opportunity to speak into the methods and means of this new church. They often suggest things that seem surprisingly different, but not theologically unsound. These fresh voices simply aren't caught in the "we've always done it this way before" liturgy. Instead, their response is built out of their own creativity and the perceived functionality needed. In addition, they want church to be fun, not simply experienced out of duty or obligation. So, they make recommendations, accordingly.

To be sure, new churches are usually started and led by more artistic minds. They are visionaries (often "dreamers" is a more appropriate word), who tend toward story-telling, and prefer visual methods of transmitting the Gospel and making disciples. They are spontaneous, less predictable, and love variety. They are intuitive problem solvers. They love aesthetics, and they seek to bring beauty and art back into the life of the church. Moreover, they believe one of the cardinal rules in church life is this: Thou shalt not be boring. Since God is never boring, how can church fail to be the same?

In some ways, they have never left the values and methods of their adolescence. They know these things engaged a tough audience at the most distracted of times in life. Yet, the unconventional nature of life as a teen resonates with those in adulthood who are bored and uninterested in a "vanilla-only" church. They attempt to speak to a Neapolitan world through a variety of means that are unpredictable, thought-provoking, engaging, and relevant to life today in the 21st century.

The creativity of these new churches is expressed in a variety of ways, from the names they take to the places they meet. They differ dramatically in the ways they worship to how they live out church life the rest of the week. Why? It is because they believe it truly does take all kinds of churches to reach all kinds of people. So they build bridges to the unique audience God has enabled them to engage, and they eliminate barriers of image and culture that can keep that same audience away.

Finally, effective new churches live with a constant Kingdom orientation.[13] This is hugely important, for they never lose sight of two important facts: every kingdom has a king, and no single castle makes up the kingdom.

These new churches are fixated on their King. They are determined to serve Him to the best of their ability and to the extent of their potential. They constantly remind the people that Jesus is the Head of the church, not the pastor or its board. As such, they are constantly orientating themselves to Him and aligning themselves as His people with His own heart. Their citizenship is in heaven (Philippians 3:20), and their allegiance belongs there, too.

As citizens they are part of a larger entity—the people of God—a nation of brothers and sisters in Christ whose identity transcends brand names or labels. While many—perhaps most—church planters are part of denominations and/or networks, they serve in such tribes because of the deeply held belief that in so doing, they are able to accomplish the mission more effectively. Part of this is found in the resourcing the tribe brings to bear upon the new congregation. But part of it is found in the relationships discovered and its corollary reminder: no one does this ministry alone. We have Christ, and we have each other.

Kingdom Orientation: Effective churches never lose sight of two important facts: every kingdom has a king, and no single castle makes up the kingdom.

Led by visionaries, new churches constantly see the big picture off the horizon and refuse to forget that their ministry is a part of a larger whole. Their church plant is but a portion of all God is doing in and through His people to further His kingdom's work. Consequently, church planters experience the synergy, evangelistic impact, and kingdom advance made possible by such a perspective. A macro-view keeps them from diminishing the work of God to just one church start.

As a result, these planters form creative alliances and networks that transcend tribe and denomination, all for the sake of Christ and His kingdom. They keep their eyes on the mission, and they find willing allies who also desire to advance His cause. One might think this would hinder a new church's commitment and viability, or that it would be counter-intuitive to focus on the kingdom and not simply on their church. However, beyond the supernatural blessing of God that should be obvious in such cases, these new churches find just the opposite: passionate vitality enthused within their congregation and community companions, cooperating around the larger mission of making disciples, whenever, wherever, and however they can.

This cooperation serves as the cornerstone of the synergy experienced and the evidence of a congregational heart that demonstrates a dependence on God. It is this humility that unites the people of God and transcends tribal lines for the as-yet-unreached community to see. It is the power of love that reminds everyone that this is Christ's church, and He is the head. With a focus like this on the kingdom of God, effective new churches remind those they reach that all they do is constantly based on the Lord's agenda, not their own.

These five defining characteristics, then, are a critical part of what makes new churches start so effectively. They help the new church stay healthy and strong. In particular, these characteristics cause the new church to get out into the world around them. It provides them the exercise they need to continue their growth properly. It is the out-growth of the in-working God's Spirit is doing in their hearts. To this end, new churches use these principles to stay focused on evangelism and disciple-making, which is at the center of the mission given by Christ.

But none of these characteristics will necessarily result in health and growth, unless they are built upon the proper foundations. It is to this we next turn our attention.

APPLY TO YOUR SETTING

1. Which of these characteristics is our church doing effectively at this time? What makes them so effective? What can we learn from our successes?

2. Which of these characteristics is most challenging to our church at this time? Why? What lessons can we learn from this?

3. What one new (really, old) thing should we try next to help us begin to see and experience our life as the church together the way we did in our earliest years?

4. How can the advantages of age and wisdom, resources and experience assist us in applying this effort, rather than keeping us from it?

5. What do we need to do to "re-learn" our community? Who do we need to meet? What do we need to read or find? What do we need to experience?

6. How are we enhancing relationships and helping them to grow?

QUESTIONS TO CONSIDER

1. What would we be willing to try if we knew we could not fail?

2. What keeps us from innovating or trying new things to reach new people? Attitudes? Fears?

3. What is our priority in ministry: people, programs, facilities, something else? Why?

DIGGING DEEPER

Birch, Rich. **Unreasonable Churches.** Middletown, DE: unSeminary, 2016.

Christopherson, Jeff. **The Kingdom Matrix, expanded edition.** Boise, ID: Elevate Faith, 2016.

Gumbel, Nicky. **The Alpha Course manual**, 2nd edition. London: Alpha Books, 2004.

Holladay, Tom. **The Relationship Principles of Jesus.** Grand Rapids, MI: Zondervan Publishing House, 2009.

Hunter III, George G. **The Celtic Way of Evangelism: Tenth Anniversary edition.** Nashville, TN: Abingdon Press, 2010.

Jackson, J. David. **PLANTED.** Severn, MD: Screven and Allen Publishing, 2012.

Mittleberg, Mark. **Building a Contagious Church.** Grand Rapids, MI: Zondervan Publishing House, 2000.

Rusaw, Rick and Swanson, Eric. **The Externally-Focused Church.** Loveland, CO: Group Publishing, 2004.

Sjogren, Steven. **101 Ways to Reach Your Community.** Colorado Springs, CO: NavPress, 2001.

~ 26 ~

FOUNDATIONAL FACTORS

Pastor Stephen had watched Redemption Fellowship, the new church in town, grow steadily over its first year. He was amazed at the progress they had made! Everywhere he went, there was evidence of this new church. They were visible in town affairs and community activities. They were developing creative and unique ways to inform the townspeople about Jesus and their new church. Pastor Joe, their leader, had taken the initiative to build relationships with other pastors and community leaders who wanted to see poverty eliminated in the town and education strengthened.

Stephen also noticed how effectively they were building relationships with the townspeople. They seemed to have groups and gatherings in all the neighborhoods and for many different reasons. At first, Pastor Stephen's reaction to this was defensive. "They will affect our ministry at First Church," he thought. "They might even take people away from our church," he worried. But then he recognized the efforts of Redemption Fellowship were not focused on the people already at his church—or any church, for that matter. They were connecting with people at bars, casinos, and even the racetrack.

His amazement mingled with frustration. "I wish the attendees at First Church lived like those at Redemption Fellowship," he concluded. "I wonder why they are so different from us?"

Pastor Stephen scheduled a meeting with Pastor Joe,

in an attempt to unpack the reasons why this new church was so effective. The new pastor welcomed the opportunity to meet with Stephen, and in his own words, "to learn from someone who has been here many years and knows his way around." As he listened to Pastor Joe talk about Redemption Fellowship's vision to reach the community and how focused they were on the mission God had given them, he wondered if Joe's words were true.

Did he "know his way around" the town? Had he forgotten the important keys that unlocked ministry for First Church in years past? As Pastor Joe continued and talked of the new church's sense of calling and the motivating factors behind "why they do what they do," Pastor Stephen found himself asking the same question of his own church. He discovered that Redemption Fellowship had a lean, nimble infrastructure, which enabled them to respond quickly and effectively to ministry opportunities that surfaced. He also noted that they made sure that their calendar and budget stayed focused on the mission and vision of Redemption Fellowship, and nothing else.

Of course, Pastor Stephen couldn't help but admire his colleague and new friend, Pastor Joe. He was an inspiring man. He spoke with conviction and decisiveness. He had passion and joy. He exuded enthusiasm and excitement. It didn't take long to determine this young man had great faith and was willing to follow God anywhere. "It's no wonder the people of Redemption Fellowship live the way they live," he surmised. "Their pastor is just like that himself."

I grew up in a suburb of New Orleans, Louisiana, during my teenage years. If you know much about New Orleans, you know it is a unique place with a special personality all its own. Like every city, it has its attractions and its detractions. It is fun and it is dangerous. It is eccentric and it is erratic. Regardless, for me it was home.

Much of southern Louisiana faces two perennial problems: annual hurricane concerns and swampy, sinking soil underfoot. As a teenager, I regularly witnessed both. Almost every summer-into-early fall, we would have to "batten down the hatches of our home" and head to a storm shelter, in order to endure a hurricane or tropical storm. My wife, Joyce, and I even had to contend with one at our wedding! In addition, every few years we had to add soil to the land upon which our house was built, because the ground (but not our house) was sinking beneath us.

When new homes were built down Jeannette Drive where we lived, I discovered the secret to their survival. Long, strong pylons of wood and metal were literally machine-hammered fifty feet into the ground. These pylons gripped the ground deep below the surface and provided the necessary stability upon which to build a structure. In essence, they formed the basis for the essential foundation of the soon-to-be-built house. These pylons were never seen again, yet their presence enabled the inhabitants of that new house to live and function as intended. Without the pylons, though, their existence, and that of their dwelling place, would sooner or later be in grave danger.

Such is the existence of churches. Their lives must be built upon a firm foundation. Jesus is the cornerstone of such a foundation for His church. With His leadership, our Lord shapes each church uniquely, but with the same necessary pylons to undergird the ministry they have. Like longtime residents of a dwelling place, these invisible elements at work in the experience of a church may be easily forgotten or dismissed. They may be ignored or neglected, because when they are functioning properly they fail to draw attention to themselves.

However, if something goes wrong in the unseen world undergirding the work of Christ, it becomes evident in the structure itself. Cracks in the foundation jeopardize everything the church is here to do! Because of this reality, care must be taken to visit and revisit the stability of this foundation regularly. After all, the foundation has a way of shaping how we live our lives; its influence on our existence is far-reaching.

This is true of every church. However, many established churches have forgotten, or even worse, have ignored these foundations. Perhaps this occurs because those who are a part of the church now are not those who laid the foundation at the beginning. Later inhabitants often assume their predecessors took care of these foundational issues, and thus, feel no need to address them. In other instances, though, established churches fail to see the value of such things and instead, attempt to only beautify the structure above ground. While this helps in one sense, it also functions more like the proverbial bandage to the issue or need; it fails to address the most basic of questions: why.

THE FOUNDATION EVERY CHURCH REQUIRES

Foundational issues, or internal, unseen characteristics, form the basis of effective new churches. In *PLANTED: Starting Well, Growing Strong*, I identified five internal elements that enable a new church to be effective and evangelistic in impacting the people around it. Along with the five external factors mentioned in the previous chapter (what we do), these characteristics (why we do what we do) are the significant reasons new churches have such dramatic success in their earliest years.

First, a new church is birthed out of a calling from God.[14] This calling is personal, unique, and special. It is seen first in the life of the planter and is exemplified in his personality and lifestyle. But over time, "the mirror principle" teaches that the congregation will own the calling, as well. They will develop a unique personality based on this calling and it will be seen in their corporate lifestyle, from how they experience worship to how they minister in the community.

> **The Calling of God: Effective churches...chose to define success in terms of faithfulness and obedience to God, period. They trust God to take care of the rest.**

This calling, if it is genuine and God-given, will provide the proper motivation to catalyze the work forward. Based upon the grace of God and His love for people, new churches are shaped in ways that will evidence the mercy, acceptance, and forgiveness of God. Impure motives, like fame, simply providing an alternative option, running away from something, or even success, will not stand the test of time. In fact, effective planters and their churches refuse to accept the standard of the world as their own definition of "success." Rather than numbers or attention received, they choose to define success in terms of faithfulness and obedience to God, period. They trust God to take care of the rest.

The abandonment to God is obvious, and its sociological reason is evident: there is a sense of desperation in what they are doing. Their very survival depends upon the church taking root and becoming established over these early years. If it does not become viable, then their livelihood is over, and the effort will have fallen short of expectations and investment. So, desperation fuels their activity and efforts. But if the calling is pure and holy, the desperation is not out of panic or self-image concerns, but rather out of faith and wholehearted submission to, and dependence upon, God.

Planters remember all the time that this is, after all, God's work. Christ is the head of the church. And no one—no one—cares about this church more than Jesus does.

Second, effective new churches are also catalyzed forward by the vision of God.[15] This vision is not simply something the church planter feels or wants to accomplish. Rather, it is the revealed desire of God for this new church, and as such, forms the foundation for the identity of the church plant and the way it will live out its existence in the years to come. Effective church planters understand this not simply to be a vision from God, but the vision of God, for their church and its community of influence.

> **The Vision of God: Effective churches understand this is not simply a vision from God, but the vision of God, for their church and its community of influence.**

Such a vision seems to pull them into the future, where it can become reality. This is highly important and easily done, since they have no past to seduce them. The vision ignites them, guides them, safeguards them, and eventually evaluates them. Because this is true, the people of this new church must value the vision. They have to own the vision and protect the vision from erosion or neglect. As they own it, they share it with others who will do the same. They understand this vision to be a personal glimpse of God's heart for them, and His first and primary message to them. It is the Good News embodied through them for their mission field.

Consequently, they understand this not as a marketing campaign or a way to "rally the troops." It fuels their identity and purpose in existence. So they become single-minded in their focus and determination to accomplish God's will for them. They refuse to let anything sidetrack them or deter them from its achievement. They persevere.

Over time, the temptation to add more and more activity can dilute the focus and single-mindedness of the new church regarding the vision. So instead, the church plant uses the vision to filter the activity of the church, making sure everything they do and the subsequent energy and resources expended help the church move toward the fulfillment of the vision. They also use it to filter the membership of the church, so that all those who become a part of the new church plant family adopt this vision, and not a competing one, as their own.

Third, effective new churches build an internal structure that facilitates the above.[16] Simply put, the structures of the new church stay simple and functional. This is done informally at first in the earliest days, as decisions and personnel all aim to accomplish the vision. Over time the structure is formalized in some ways, but still is kept small, simple and clear, so that the new church can be quick in response to needs and concerns that arise.

Functional Structure: Effective churches structure for impact. They build a culture of trust and empower people to move out into ministry.

This is contrary to human nature. Rather than add more and more to the structure, they pare away what is unneeded in helping them accomplish the vision. They believe that less is more (*i.e.*, less bureaucracy provides more ministry). Opportunities are not lost because the system fails to allow the congregation to join God in His work as it becomes evident.

As a result, they structure for impact. They build a culture of trust and empower people to move out into ministry that will enable the congregation to make progress toward God's vision for them. They provide support, encouragement, training, and love; in addition, they offer the priceless gift of "permission" to those who are eager to serve. They structure not to restrict, but to provide opportunity and means for this kind of ministry to happen.

Part of the reason this is so effective in new churches is because they help people discover how they have been shaped by God for ministry. As newcomers uncover these realities, church leaders equip them and place them in ministry opportunities that fit their gifting and spiritual "make up." New churches hold to a theology that believes God sends the church exactly the people needed to accomplish what He has in mind, and not necessarily what the church has been doing previously. Because of this, the new church adapts its ministry to the people, not the people to its ministry. Ministries can change as long as they move us forward toward the accomplishment of the vision of God.

This causes effective new churches to function more as a family than a business. Every person is valued for his or her contribution. Every person is important. And in a highly relational environment, people are affirmed and encouraged every step of the way. While the congregation will have varying roles and gifting, there is little need to follow manuals of order or sophisticated processes; instead, they function more like fathers, mothers, sons, and daughters to one another. Decisions in this kind of environment are typically made easily and with great consensus.

Fourth, effective new churches will organize their budget and calendar around the very same priorities.[17] They are mindful of the mission of God and the part they play in bringing it to fruition in their own community. They make sure the participation and involvement of their people in activity is centered on the things that will keep them focused on the mission and enable them to make progress toward the achievement of the vision. New churches resource their activities financially in the same way, by the same plumb line. They must enable the church to move forward strategically, not in an aimless or wasteful way.

To this end, a large portion of their man hours and dollars are geared toward evangelism and outreach. Upwards of twenty-five percent of their income is directed this way, with as much as fifty percent used on outreach in year one. This keeps the focus on reaching people with the Gospel and growing the church, which in turn enables it to have greater impact, near and far.

Both near and far are important, for the new church seeks to make a difference, not only in its immediate neighborhood, but also around the world. It sacrifices to serve in far away places, not just through its gifts but through the calendaring of mission trips to distant places where the Gospel is dimly known. This priority has an inverse affect upon the new congregation as a whole, for those who return from the mission field, come back changed, revitalized, and more passionate than ever about God and His work. Accordingly, these benefits spill over into the life of the new church and infuse it with more energy, excitement, and passion to reach their world for Jesus. Effective new churches truly believe they can change the world, for Jesus' sake.

Budget and Calendar for Priorities: Effective new churches believe they can change the world for Jesus' sake. To do this, they keep fixed expenses to a minimum.

How are they able to budget so much for outreach? How are they able to sacrifice so much for missions? In a word, the answer is priorities. These are the lifeblood of an effective new church. To this end, they keep fixed expenses to a minimum. For example, they usually rent or lease for many years. This saves them an on-going mortgage, utility bills, and maintenance expenses. They have limited staff and personnel, and those they have are usually underpaid, by society's standards. Typically, staffers willingly accept the limitations, because the mission is more important. Limiting these fixed expenses enables more resources to be available for others to discover Jesus.

More than anything else, though, the new church is effective because it has an inspiring—and courageous—leader.[18] This planter is different by nature from your typical pastor. He is an initiator of relationships and activity, not a manager or a reactor in the same situations. He is creative and outgoing, and while he will be a jack-of-many-trades in church ministry, he is an equipper and empower-er of others. He sees the big picture and is a visionary, but is able to encourage and motivate the least visible person in the flock. In gifting he is not a pastoral care-giver, but rather, an effective communicator and team leader, who will engage others with the vision, enable them to own it, and will celebrate their successes along the way. He believes in prayer and lives a life of faith, hope, and love that inspires others to join him on the journey. As a result, many do.

This "Pied Piper" effect is critical to the new church's success, as it builds significant momentum that cascades over time. There is high energy, enthusiasm, and excitement everywhere, borne out of the optimism and strong belief in God to provide what is needed in every situation of life. This attitude is contagious and energetic to the people, who are willing to "expect great things from God and attempt great things for God."

Over time, this attitude is exemplified in the life of the congregation as a whole. Usually, by the time the new church's second birthday rolls around, the church is mirroring the attitudes and values of their founding pastor, this special man who has been their church planter. During the subsequent formative years in the new church's life, these values, attitudes, and priorities are solidified if the church planter stays. They will form the basis for a growing church in the decade yet to come.

Inspiring—and Courageous—Leadership: Effective churches will face obstacles and adversaries, and must act with tenacity, strength, and conviction in love.

This "mirroring effect" is different in the life of an established church, though. Gary McIntosh, author and professor of Christian Ministry and Leadership at Talbot School of Theology, once told me that for an established church, it takes a pastor at least seven years to experience this reality.[19] As a result, the pastor of an established church must do more than inspire; he must act with courage and determination. In fact, more than any other characteristic mentioned so far, this one differs for established church pastors from what is needed in church planters.[20] While church planters must inspire their congregation, established church pastors intent upon renewal must inspire and at the same time, be courageous. They will face obstacles and adversaries unknown in the church planting environment and must act with tenacity, strength, and conviction in love.

Their courage will likely cost them something—friends, resources, influence. Sacrifice is an inevitable part of the renewal pastor's lot. But the reward is great. The longsuffering, courageous pastor can reap a new harvest, forge a new path for the congregation, and experience eternal dividends for the Kingdom. They hold firmly to the promise of God, *"Let us not grow tired of doing good, for we will reap at the proper time if we don't give up"* (Galatians 6:9).

These five additional, internal characteristics form the foundation for the new church's existence and activity. They give shape to the identity of the church and value to all who are a part. They establish the basis for what is done and the boundaries for what is not done. They give focus, clarity, and simplicity to its work. In addition, they place the value of the church on the people—not the programs, or the facility, or anything else. This is its strength. For as long as the new church concentrates its life on these things, it makes forward progress, because its foundation is strong.

Established churches can do these things very well; likely they did in their earlier years. Many have just forgotten their value and thus, fail to understand their importance. Reengaging the congregation around such meaningful elements in the church's existence are critical for future progress. They keep the church from sinking in a time of shifting sand.

APPLY TO YOUR SETTING

1. Which of these characteristics is our church doing effectively at this time? What makes them so effective? What can we learn from our successes?

2. Which of these characteristics is most challenging to our church at this time? Why? What lessons can we learn from this?

3. What were the foundational elements of our church when it started: its calling, vision, and focus? How have they changed over the years? What are they currently?

4. How is our understanding of these things reflected in our budget and our calendar of events? What do these tools say about us and our priorities?

5. How does our structure help us (or hurt us) in advancing the work of Christ in and through the church? What needs to change?

6. How is our pastor like an effective church planter? How is he different?

QUESTIONS TO CONSIDER

1. What does God see when He looks at our church? At our community? What does He want?

2. How desperate are we to serve God as His church, "whatever it takes?" What might temper our passion?

3. If the future of the church depended on me, what would it look like?

#renewbook

DIGGING DEEPER

Allen, Roland. **Missionary Methods: St. Paul's or Ours?** Grand Rapids, MI: Eerdmans, 1962.

Guinness, Os. **The Call.** Nashville, TN: W Publishing, 2003.

Harrell, Jim, **Church Replanter.** Rowley, MA: Overseed Press, 2014.

Malphurs, Aubrey. **Being Leaders**. Grand Rapids, MI: Baker Books, 2003.

Moore, Ralph. **Starting a New Church.** Ventura, CA: Regal Books, 2002.

Nebel, Tom and Rohrmayer, Gary. **Church Planting Landmines.** Carol Stream, IL: ChurchSmart Resources, 2005.

Stanley, Andy. **Visioneering**. Sisters, OR: Multnomah Publishing, 1999.

PART

TWO

"Behold, I am Doing a New Thing…"

PREPARING FOR THE JOURNEY

Pastor Stephen had become convinced First Church could no longer "do business as usual." The church was struggling at best to keep up with the changes taking place all around them. These changes were influencing the attendees who visited the church and even those who were members for several years. In addition, the members of the congregation had become comfortable with the way things were done and the current results they were seeing at First Church. Since few individuals were committing themselves to follow Christ and fewer still were becoming an ongoing part of the church, this lack of results bothered Pastor Stephen. He knew the urgency of reaching people without Jesus around them demanded a more significant effort.

Stephen was impressed by what he was learning from Pastor Joe at Redemption Fellowship. He realized their situations were different, but their environment was essentially the same. Pastor Stephen wondered if he could adapt the principles and characteristics Redemption Fellowship used in his own church setting. How would the people respond? What might we expect as a result? He was confident the outcomes would differ in some ways, but intuitively thought it might actually help refocus them on some very important factors in ministry First Church seemed to be overlooking.

The pastor considered where he should start on this journey. With Joe's counsel and encouragement, he determined he needed to build upon the restlessness and dissatisfaction he sensed among some of the leadership in the church. "That will be easy," he concluded, "as there is much with which to be dissatisfied at First Church right now." Joe advised him to build a "coalition of the willing" next, to find those leaders who agreed changes needed to be made and were unwilling to accept the status quo any longer. Pastor Stephen knew not everyone would be happy about the suggested new direction of the church; he would prepare himself to address these concerns in advance. He also realized those whom Pastor Joe called "the gatekeepers in the church" might not even have designated titles or positions in First Church (at least not currently), but would need to be approached personally out of respect for both the importance and influence of their leadership.

Pastor Joe reminded Stephen that this would require patient perseverance and a whole lot of prayer. It would most likely take time for the key people in the church to get on board. "It's okay," Pastor Joe said, attempting to calm Stephen's concerns. "God is in control; trust Him to work on their hearts. Remember, He cares about His church more than any of you do."

In addition, Joe reminded Stephen his own credibility and trustworthiness would be on the line in the changes-yet-to-come. "It takes courage to lead," Stephen thought, "but God is in this, so I must take the next step forward."

If I can be confessional for a moment, I will admit I have "wanderlust." By this I mean, I fantasize often about traveling and seeing other parts of the world. In the last 24 hours, my wife Joyce and I have talked about a new and unexpected journey we may take this fall to Central Europe. Just the thought of it excites me.

For some, though, I know, travel doesn't evoke the same reaction. Some get anxious, with sweaty palms and minds filled with worry over the cost, the safety, the home front while away, and "what if" scenarios travel can bring. Others dream constantly, but are paralyzed into inactivity and indecision by the perplexity of the possibilities. Still others don't want to travel at all.

If you are going to lead your church back to the secret successes of its beginning, then you will have to take a journey. It may not be easy, and in some ways, it may be costly. It may take a long time to complete. However, it will be memorable, significant, and difference-making for you and for others. It will change the way you see yourself and the rest of the world. It will be an adventure of epic proportions!

In this book, the analogy of a journey will suggest to us readers what we must do to regain the traction of momentum and growth overviewed earlier in the life of new churches. After all, the first few years of your church must have gone well, since your church is still here after these many years. Something the founders and charter members did, they implemented correctly, and it made a big difference. While it is not possible to recover the moment in time that made the start of your church successful, it may be possible to reintroduce the factors responsible for your church's early growth and success. And that might change the trajectory of its future for years, maybe even decades, to come.

When I travel, there are some necessary prerequisites I must take to ready myself for the trip. I acknowledge my desire to travel and determine to do something about it. I coordinate my trip with my calendar and colleagues. I determine who else wants to travel with me. I educate and prepare both those going with me and those staying behind for the anticipated adjustments the trip will bring to their lives. I secure the necessary documentation for the trip. I map out my destination and the itinerary needed to get me there.

This analogy provides many similarities in dealing with a church when attempting to help it advance in growth, move off the plateau, or reverse its decline. Each situation is different and unique; however, there are some commonalities in experience and process that can prepare the church for what is ahead. It is to these items that we now turn our attention.

"NOW IS THE WINTER OF OUR DISCONTENT"

When William Shakespeare wrote these words in the

play, *The Tragedy of Richard the Third*, over five hundred years ago,[21] he wasn't talking about the church you serve. In fact, unless the budget is strained because income is precipitously low, or lay leadership is unhappy with the pastor (for any number of reasons), there is probably very little discontent within your church. This is unfortunate in some ways, since discontent with the status quo is necessary for significant change to take place. John Kotter, in his classic work on this topic, *Leading Change*, lists this as fundamental to the process of moving forward.[22] Just as in travel, you will never go elsewhere until you are certain it will be more beneficial than simply staying where you are, so it is in church life, too. There must be discontent with the status quo for any church—maybe even any group or organization—to desire and then implement change.

There must be discontent with the status quo for any church—maybe even any group or organization—to desire and then implement change.

Why is this? Scholars suggest a large majority of human beings are creatures of habit. We change these habits out of necessity or need almost intuitively; however, we rarely change these habits out of choice, unless the alternative offers us significant desired benefits.[23] Once changes are implemented, humans want the security found in routine. Simply put, change creates stress; routine gives comfort. Too much stress and humans will resist or withdraw from it, if possible.

If an established church is in decline or has plateaued, it must first desire to reverse the trend. While leaders are often change agents or more desirable of change than followers (*i.e.*, the majority in any church),[24] even pastors rarely implement change simply for the sake of change. Rather, there is an obvious, functional reason that provokes leaders to desire change over the status quo. In the situation at hand, it is the decline in membership or influence that typically prompts the consideration of change. However, even then it is rarely more than a suggestion or consideration unless one of two things happens: the current scenario gets radically worse or the benefits on the other side of change get increasingly more attractive.

In most churches with which I have worked over the years, neither of these situations has occurred. The congregation listens willingly with their head to the information shared about the process, the potential results, and even the requirements necessary to make such a change happen. However, the heart is not in it; the church is just not "there" yet. Most are simply curious, examining other alternatives for their own consideration. Until they become convinced of the necessity, churches will not change.

This typically happens when desperation rises to an uncomfortable level. The bills are not being paid, the bank account is almost empty, the facilities are becoming unusable, people have left in large numbers and only a few remain: these kind of situations prompt leaders to consider something new that requires change. This is even less likely to happen if the collective past of the church is storied and significant. Members will not easily give up the past, since it is a part of their own identity.

On the other hand, the potential benefits may entice people to change, but not typically among those you already have within the church. It is a mistake to assume the people within your church want to grow. Sure, they would like to reach enough outsiders to ease their conscience regarding the reason the church exists. Certainly, they also want to reach enough people to relieve their concerns about the budget and the volunteer leaders needed for on-going programming in the church.

The longer the tenured leadership and average member have been a part of the church, the less likely they are to desire change at all.

But these benefits are rarely enough to motivate members to desire the change necessary to reclaim the growth patterns of the past. In fact, the longer the tenured leadership and average member have been a part of the church, the less likely they are to desire change at all, unless the church is literally at the point of death.

Now if you are reading this book, then I'm assuming

you are at least curious about what it will take to move your church forward in the months and years ahead. If I am correct in assuming this, then I must counsel you further: until you are desperate enough to lead major change in the life of the church, you are wasting your time. This is not for the faint of heart! It will require great courage and bold risk-taking. It will involve difficult decisions and will not be popular with some of your congregation. It will demand sacrifice, and it will leave scars. Moreover, it is not a quick fix, and for it to last, it requires your commitment to longevity in serving your church. Even then, there's no guarantee your efforts will succeed.

If you are still reading and haven't abandoned the determination to help the church reverse its trajectory, then I commend you. I am guessing you sense God leading you in this, that it is a calling you must follow. Church planters feel this way about the work they start from scratch. You must be just as convinced this is what God calls you to do. This is His heart and His desire, and you seek to be obedient to this call. I affirm this response with every ounce of my being! If this is truly what God wants, then He will lead you every step of the way.

However, if this is not a calling from God, then check your motivations. Church planters "wash out" because they want a preferred way of church methodology, a desire for fame, a way to validate their esteem issues, or to prove something to someone else. So, ask God to *"Search me...and know my heart; test me and know my concerns. See if there is any offensive way in me"* (Psalm 139:23-24a). If there is, revisit your motivations until they are pure and pleasing to God. After all, we must never forget: this is all about Him, not you or me.

For those who feel called of God to proceed, understanding how change happens in the life of people will help. Many years ago, I was introduced to the Holmes and Rahe Stress Scale that proposes certain experiences in life create significant levels of stress in our lives here on earth. All of these items are the product of change we encounter.[25] The theory behind the list is this: the greater the change, positive or negative, the more stress it generates. Higher levels of stress experienced over lengthy periods of time can cause adverse physical reaction (*i.e.*, the body starts to break down).

This is true in church life, too. While no one has ever created such a list of stressors for church congregations (at least, not that I'm aware of), the theory holds true corporately, as well: people can only handle so much stress (and the change that produces it) at any given time. Add to this the psychological dynamics that suggest change is contrary to most personality types, and you have a high probability of adverse reactions. People even prefer to live in a "frog in the kettle" situation, rather than suffer through radical change.[26]

For leaders, then, timing is everything. They must know when it is best to address this issue, as well as how to address it. This is why the "season of discontent" is so important. If the congregation is stressed over other changes happening in its life that are dramatically changing the landscape of the corporate church experience as they know it, then the changes suggested here may be seen as a positive solution. This has its own built-in motivating factor. It will cause the church to see the growth alternative as a benefit, not a concern.

More times than not, though, a congregation is "at ease in Zion" and complacent or apathetic about the key concerns leadership faces. In these instances, the pastor and leaders may need to give members greater reasons to be restless and uncomfortable in their current situation. This may sound callous and harsh, but in reality it is not. This is actually a biblical process used over and over again, to stir people out of their complacency and on to godly objectives.

It is correct and it is biblical to "turn up the heat" on complacency and apathy.

Consider the children of Israel at Kadesh-Barnea. Upon refusing the forward command of God to take the Promised Land, God through Moses pronounced judgment upon that generation and moved the people forward only after completing the promised judgment on all who failed to obey Him (Numbers 13-14). Or how about Joshua? He challenged the people to *"Choose for yourselves today: which will you worship?"* (Joshua 24:15). And there was Elijah, who also challenged the people about whom they would serve, for *"If the LORD is God, follow Him; but if Baal, follow him"* (1 Kings 18:21). Of course, there was our Savior Jesus, too. After feeding 5000, according to John's Gospel, He gave a striking sermon, saying *"Unless you eat the flesh of the Son of Man and drink His blood, you do not have life in yourselves. The one who eats my flesh and drinks my blood has eternal life,"* for those who would follow Him. This made many so uncomfortable, that they turned away from following Him (John 6:43-66).

In other words, it is correct and it is biblical to "turn up the heat" on complacency and apathy. God calls upon us to challenge His people to a higher standard than convenience and comfort. So what are the ways this can be done?

Some positive motivating factors include:

- God's love for the lost around us
- The power of the Gospel to change lives
- The reason we exist
- Our responsibility to be obedient
- God's grace we have experienced
- God's grace others need to experience
- The extension of the church's impact
- Our Lord's pleasure with us

Some negative motivating factors include:

- Not living out our mission
- Accountability before God
- The gains of Satan in our society
- The neglect of others who depend on us
- Our selfishness and pride
- Our lack of care about those without Jesus
- The church's imminent death or loss of influence
- The church's inability to survive (attract people, pay bills)
- The transmission of ineffective discipleship to the next generation

The pastor and leaders have to facilitate an environment that embraces the need to move forward toward this calling of God to grow and reach out effectively once more. They need to agree upon how to approach this effort with the people as a whole.

Timing is also affected by the pastor's own experience and longevity within the church. For church planters, it typically takes two years for the congregation to start mirroring the values, attitudes, and lifestyle of the new pastor. However, for established churches this can take much longer. Scholars have argued that seven years is a significant time for the tenure of pastors in church life.[27] In other words, when pastors of established churches pass seven years of ministry with the same congregation, they have usually garnered enough credibility, trust, and influence to lead the church in significant change, with little or no resistance. This is probably an important consideration for most pastors to keep in mind.

There is another option, however. It is possible to attempt a radical change during the honeymoon period (the first two years) of the pastor's arrival at his post. This is possible because the pastor is held in high esteem by most of the people in the congregation. (He hasn't been humanized yet.) He is granted a great deal of trust and latitude during this stage, as well. Because of this, he can change things with less repercussions. (Please note I said "less," rather than "no" repercussions.) But be forewarned: while there is less chance radical change during this early period will end in abrupt termination, it will certainly end the honeymoon period prematurely. In addition, the new pastor's trust and credibility may take a long time to re-establish. In the meantime, he and his family may experience a great deal of loneliness and absence of support.

How does a leader decide which approach to take? He must know himself and his congregation. In knowing himself, he understands how his personality type will affect the responses of those who are a part of the church. He also recognizes the "trust factor" he has with the people inside the church. In knowing the congregation, he is aware of how they react to change and to him as their leader. He also knows timing in the church's life makes a huge difference in their readiness to follow.

A COALITION OF THE WILLING

John Kotter's other key contribution to the change experience in group life is the recognition that leaders must build a coalition of the willing.[28] In other words, after creating discontent with the status quo, the leader must find allies who support the anticipated change.

A smart leader is one who knows his congregation well enough to realize who the "gatekeepers" are in the life of the church. The leader understands these are the key influencers and decision-makers in the congregation. He knows that titles and positions of responsibility in the church do not necessarily reveal the people who can open the doors to suggested change among the life of God's people. Moreover, as we have already stated, unless the pastor himself has been a part of the church for over seven years, then he is probably not the top influencer himself.

To gain support of the hoped-for change, wise leaders will meet one-on-one with these gatekeepers to discuss the decision. Symptoms, consequences (positive and negative), and results need to be shared. The pastor needs to find out what the concerns and objections are to the proposed change from each gatekeeper. He may not have to respond to them at this time, but he will likely have to assess their impact and respond to them later. So, it is smart to have these key individuals express their concern, if they are willing.

If these gatekeepers are people who accept change easily, this experience will be more informational in purpose. The pastor will discover allies to leverage the congregation, when dealing with this coming change. However, some gatekeepers will resist the change. Sometimes this is because they are people who don't like change in life, period. Other times it is because they will disagree with the specific change proposed. However, the elephant in the room with gatekeepers is change may diminish their role with the congregation, and most people who fit this reality will resist this happening.

This is why it's important to meet with these

gatekeepers one-on-one. This dilutes their influence upon the group or congregation as a whole, at least until the pastor knows where each of these key individuals stands on the issue. Only after these gatekeepers have been heard individually should the pastor present the proposed growth change strategy to the rest of the leadership. With key gatekeepers already on board, the likelihood of the change being derailed is significantly lowered. Finally, the entire congregation should be approached with the change initiative; this should be the final stage in the presentation process.

Pastors are well-advised to know even after all these meetings have happened a quick, affirmative response may not take place. Typically, groups of people, including organizations and churches, have a predictable way of responding to change opportunities. Many years ago (1962), Professor Everett Rogers in his book *Diffusion of Innovations* popularized this theory when he developed a bell graph that illustrates this well.[29] About sixteen percent of those affected will readily embrace the change presented to them. Another sixteen percent or so will resist the change no matter what. However, the other sixty-eight percent will accept the change, if given enough time to process it appropriately.

This is not because they necessarily approve of the change itself. Rather, it is because they have been given the time needed to come to grips with the change and to have confidence in their leader. If their concerns are heard and they trust their leader, in most instances they will follow, regardless of their personal opinion on the matter.

This is significant. Leaders must be confident and trustworthy; they must know their flock, listen to them, and have credibility with them. When possible, they must give them time to assess and accept the necessary change. This may take weeks, months or in some instances, even years. But they must not wait for everyone to get on board; in most instances, especially ones of great magnitude and emotional investment, that is never going to happen.

At some point, the leader must lead and move ahead with the sense of calling God has given to him in this regard. For the initiative to have a great chance to succeed, the pastor must have built a large coalition of the willing who will support the endeavor. He must have also minimized the chance those opposed to the proposed change will attempt to sabotage or undermine the effort by promoting divisions in the church.

TWO OTHER ISSUES THAT MUST BE ADDRESSED

Every church has guiding documents and/or precedents that advise the process of decision-making. In *PLANTED: Starting Well, Growing Strong*, I share that new churches with limited structure are more effective in making forward Kingdom movement in growth and evangelism.[30] This is because they are nimbler and quicker to respond to opportunities in ministry, due to the lack of bureaucracy and procedures required to gain the needed approval. While we will look at the challenges these guiding documents and precedents create in a later chapter, suffice it to say now these items suggest a process for dealing with major shifts in ministry and congregational lifestyle. Because this is true, the pastor needs to consult these documents and precedents to know procedurally how to move forward and secure official approval from the church.

Church government and polity will differ from one denomination to another, and often within these denominations there are variations on the process, as well. The pastor needs to be well-versed in the system for the church with whom he is serving; he should understand the ins-and-outs of the decision-making process, in particular. Every effort should be made to follow the procedure in place to gain approval. If the system needs to be changed, deal with it long before the recommended growth initiative comes before the governing authority for a decision.

Why? People tend to default to suspicion toward those in authority. This is human nature, at least here in the Western world. People do not want anyone infringing upon their rights (and privileges!). They refuse to let anyone stifle their voice and restrain our freedoms.

As a result, in my experience people react adversely to

two specific situations from authority in church life that impact group dynamics (by that I mean, how we all get along together as a church): attempts to change the operating procedures of the church, and silence. In the first instance, "groupthink" typically suggests such changes are not good; rather, they are self-serving. In fact, such attempted changes are often met with the default attitude that leadership wants to circumvent the approved and adopted system.

Silence is met with suspicion, too. When leaders fail to communicate and share transparently with the Body about concerns it wants addressed, people react negatively. They wonder what leaders are hiding or why they are keeping secrets. The lack of information and dialogue promotes opposition.

In the midst of emotionally-charged group decision-making moments when much is riding on the outcome, little good can come from attempting to change the system. It will be misinterpreted, and trust will erode. On the other hand, open communication will promote trust among the church toward its leaders, including the pastor. This goes a long way toward support for key decisions when they need to be made.

In addition to these operating documents and precedents that must not be ignored, the pastor of a church suggesting a new growth initiative must also reckon with the reality that he is being evaluated and compared to his predecessors. Church planters never have to deal with this scenario (unless their church starts as a result of a previous church split), so the ability to make change quickly and effectively is always possible. After all, no one predates them in the life and history of the church. They ARE its main gatekeeper and decision-maker. However, pastors of established churches are naïve to think their recommendations for change are going to be evaluated solely on their own merits. The messenger is a part of the message.

> **Pastors are naïve to think their recommendations for change are going to be evaluated solely on their merits. The messenger is a part of the message.**

Established churches often have had many pastors. Each has brought his own plans and suggestions on how to make the church more effective in the community. Some of these ideas have worked well and are remembered fondly. This is most often because of who he was, not simply because of what was done. The current pastor has to combat this "hero" in the minds of many members, since his own approach—rightly so—will be different from that of his predecessor.

Other previous pastors have not been as successful in their recommendations and approaches. Because of this, they are not remembered as fondly. Their initiatives also are tied to their persona, and thus, the initiative or method they used carries baggage with congregants because it is tied negatively in their minds to this former pastor.

As we have stated previously, it takes pastors about seven years to begin to see their values and priorities reflected in the lifestyle of the congregation. The tenures of former pastors who preceded him at the church compound this. Understanding their similar and varied approaches will help the current pastor in addressing the fears and concerns of the congregation in regards to this new growth initiative.

To many members in the church, the pastor will always be a newcomer. They will have predated him by many years (and often, many pastors!). They will have heard many of his suggestions in previous periods of church life. For some of them, they will consider such suggestions "faddish" or "not who we are." This has little to do with the current pastor himself, but rather with what has happened previously. Other members have transferred in from outside congregations, where different methods and subsequent effectiveness were experienced. As a result, their reactions may differ and their support be tepid.

Pastors do well to analyze the complexity of their congregation and lead accordingly. Those who do so with compassion and perseverance can make great strides in leading the congregation to embrace the opportunity before them. Those pastors who do not will soon hit the tripwires of personal preference and past experience, and as a result, they will not be prepared for the shrapnel that will come their way.

The ones who survive will press forward with courage, strength of character, and resolute determination. And when the decision is made to move forward, the pastor who shows such fortitude must be ready to map out the adventure ahead. It is to this concern that we turn our attention next.

APPLY TO YOUR SETTING

1. Who are the "gatekeepers" in your church? How will you approach them?

2. Who else must be in your "coalition of the willing?" How will you get them on board?

3. What positive and negative motivators are at work in your congregation right now to impact the level of discontentment that exists? How can you "turn up the fire" to highlight or enlarge the discontentment?

4. Do you have enough credibility and trust to bring about this new direction? If not, what has to change?

QUESTIONS TO CONSIDER

1. Why do you desire change? What is motivating you?

2. How do you handle stress and conflict?

3. How do patience and perseverance characterize me and my leadership style?

4. How do I primarily influence others? To enlarge my influence, what must I do?

DIGGING DEEPER

Cheyney, Tom. **The Church Revitalizer as Change Agent**. Orlando, FL: Renovate Publishing Group, 2016.

Covey, Steven. **The Speed of Trust**. New York: Free Press, 2008.

Kotter, John. **Leading Change,** revised edition. Boston: Harvard Business Review, 2012.

George, Carl F. and Logan, Robert E. **Leading and Managing Your Church.** Grand Rapids, MI: Fleming H. Revell Company, 1987.

Nelson, Alan E. and Appel, Gene. **How to Change Your Church (without Killing It).** Grand Rapids, MI: Zondervan Publishing House, 2000.

Rogers, Everett M. **Diffusion of Innovations,** 5th edition. New York: Free Press, 2003.

Schaller, Lyle. **The Change Agent.** Nashville, TN: Abingdon Press, 1994.

MAPPING THE ADVENTURE

Pastor Stephen knew he had some homework to do. He was aware of who he was and why he chose to do things in a certain way; he had a method to his own madness. However, he had come to realize that First Church also had a method of its own. Over time, it had come to prefer certain ways of doing things, essentially because those ways had worked for the church. The pastor realized that he needed to understand this "modus operandi" before he attempted to challenge it with other means or methods.

His first stop was unearthing the history of the church. Stephen read the documents he could find that told him of the significant events and persons in the church down through the years. However, he wanted to learn more than just names and dates, so he interviewed the Carltons, the Fisks, and the Ketchers, who were the remaining charter members in First Church. He also talked to the church that had sponsored their church start years ago and found a family who could remember the genesis of its beginning.

Pastor Stephen learned so much! He discovered the purpose behind the church's creation and much of what had contributed to its early success. He uncovered subsequent periods in the church's history where certain events and experiences contributed to its Kingdom impact. Through some harder work, he also unearthed its failed moments and opportunities. These he came to discover weren't written into the history for others to find. Their impact was still felt, though, nevertheless.

Knowing he needed more help in interpreting these details, Pastor Stephen studied the typical lifecycle of a church congregation. He learned that the early fifteen years or so in a church's life tend to be filled with growth opportunities. He also noted that certain decisions made later in this part of the process have long-term impact on the extension of this growth into the future. He came to understand some of the sociological dynamics in play that had caused First Church to tip precipitously downward toward decline.

Not discouraged, but well-armed with more complete knowledge, Pastor Stephen now grasped the challenge before him with both hands. "Defining reality is the first task of every leader," he thought, "but it's not the last. We must know who we are and where we are currently. But we cannot stay where we are; we must follow God's leadership into the future, a future filled with His vision of promise and possibility, of optimism and opportunity.

"As He reveals His will, we must find the ways to enable Him to use us to see it become reality. His vision must become our vision...to take us beyond where we are, to where He wants and needs us to be."

My father taught me early in life to be something of an amateur cartographer. He loved maps and taught me to value the same. We rarely seemed to stop at a service station without picking up a new map or two when we were traveling. Prior to the trip, my dad would unfold the map on the dining room table and pour over it for detail and information. He examined the available routes and evaluated the distance. He knew how long it would take us to get to our destination and where we would stop to see the sites or get a snack along the way.

I learned from my dad to do the same. From my first extensive solo journey (New Orleans to Montreal) to the move our family made from Los Angeles to Boston, I have become a student of maps. Over my lifetime, the tools have changed. No longer do I stop at a service station or even a discount retailer to buy maps; I have my computer personalize them online for my exact journey or I do this with a mapping app on my smartphone. But they still accomplish the same thing: determining my location, finding my destination, and assessing the different routes to get there.

Not having a map or failing to ask directions (hey, I am a guy, after all) has created difficulty at times for me. For churches, though, often they have been without a map for many, many years. The founding map of their church planter has been lost and other maps have failed to surface. Some churches are still using old methods to try and figure out their journey, but all the while the topography and roads around them have been changing. They may not even know where they are headed.

> **For an established church to grow, it must know both its current location and its destination.**

For an established church to grow, it must know both its current location and its destination. It will have to determine God's preferred route of travel for the congregation. It must realize they are not setting out on a tedious trip of torture, but an ambitious adventure of awesome opportunity.

These are important realizations, and they have monumental significance for the future of the church. A congregation that comes to grasp these truths has a great opportunity to recapture its future and to dream God's dream once again. But without these important discoveries, opportunities look like obstacles and significance remains stalled.

YOUR GPS

Let's review for a moment. God has placed a holy discontent within the church where you serve. It has caused people to become restless, even desperate, for something different, something better than what they are currently experiencing and sharing with the world around them. This has led you to discover God's specific calling for His church, a calling to move forward in ministry, to continue to impact the community around you evangelistically, and to grow the kingdom of God qualitatively, as well as quantitatively. You have examined your motives to be sure they are pure and honorable: this is what God wants, not simply what you want. Growth and impact are to further the fame of God, not your own. In addition, you've gained the support of the key leaders, including gatekeepers within your congregation, and formed a "coalition of the willing" who will work with you to see this calling come to fruition.

What's next? It is time to pull out your GPS and define reality. Just as a Global Positioning Satellite will reveal to you where you are currently physically located, so God's Positioning System can do the same, spiritually. It starts by hitting the "search history" marker on your touchscreen. So, it is to that priority that we now turn our attention.

If the church has had more than one pastor over the past twenty years, then chances are great that more than the current pastor is influencing the perceptions and decisions of its current life.

There are several important artifacts to uncover when dusting off the history of the church. The first and most obvious is the pastoral eras in its existence. These are highly significant, especially those that fall into two categories: those taking place during the last twenty or so years (the current generation) and that of the founding pastor (if less than fifty years ago). While these numbers are somewhat arbitrary, they represent some important facts.

If the church has had more than one pastor over the past twenty years, then chances are great that more than the current pastor is influencing the perceptions and decisions of its current life. Think of it this way: each pastor comes and builds a new layer upon the work of the previous pastor. In some instances, he continues what he finds already in place, because this fits within his values and priorities for the church. In other instances, he creates changes, for his values and priorities differ at points, too. These values and priorities, along with their visible programs and initiatives, are used by God to draw new people to the church. These new people come from two separate audiences: those who were previously unchurched and without Jesus, and those who move their membership from another church.

Those who were previously without Jesus largely perceive the pastor to be a spiritual father to them, for he loves, teaches, and disciples them. This pastor will always hold a unique and special place in their heart that no other pastor can replace. They may grow to love and appreciate another pastor more, to be sure; however, a part of their heart is reserved for the precious nature of the relationship they had with the former pastor who led them to Jesus. He has imprinted not just Jesus, but his values and priorities upon their lives.

Those who move their membership from another church are a totally different story. They may come from another church, one that did not currently satisfy their needs or wants completely. Or they may have been hurt by a church going through a number of unhealthy experiences. Their decision to stay in your church, while often motivated by God's prompting, involves evaluation and comparison of the pastor (and its programming, location, facilities, etc.) of this church with their former experiences. Depending on how long they have been "churched," they will have gone through several pastoral layers of their own at their former church that will color the way they see the values and priorities in your church. Your pastor will never be able to imprint upon their lives; at best, your pastor will influence their lives in a great way.

Church life, seen this way, is a complex web of relationships and rivaling allegiances, indeed. However, it is important for the current pastor to note not only the former pastors and the time in which they served, but also the people now in the church who arrived during their years of tenure.

Add to this a study of the major experiences, both positive and negative, that happened during the years these pastors had with the church.[31] What were the recorded successes? What brought joy to the congregation that they celebrate in their history? Recorded events will include experiences like these: significant baptism events, revivals or evangelistic services, community service impact or recognition, a school or educational enterprises, dramatic growth in attendance, the building of facilities, paying off the church debt, mission trips or efforts, and anniversaries. These are often valued and appreciated by the congregation and are, thus, written into its history.

On the other hand, negative experiences in the life of the church are rarely found in written form. They do not typically make it into the history documents of the church. These include things like these: moral failures, financial fiascoes, church splits, and the like. We will talk about this more in the next chapter of this book. For now it is best to say, a leader must put on his "investigative reporter hat" to unearth these parts of the history of the church. Typically, this means oral interviews with people, both inside and outside the church.

These former pastors and their attendant ministries join the current pastor in holding sway over the hearts and decisions of the church. Depending on how long and significant your pastoral tenure has been, the former pastors still held in high esteem within the congregation will have more or less influence over the opinions and desires of the people. Rather than fight this reality, the current pastor should leverage this by using the experiences of these local heroes of the faith in the process of moving the congregation forward from where the church currently is. As needed, reinforce valued opinions and beliefs with anecdotes and illustrations from their ministries that rally the church to support the forward-moving growth initiative.

There is a unique situation we must also mention in dealing with the history of the church; it is the life and ministry of the founding pastor. Typically, the church planter who partnered with God in starting the church, as its first pastor among other things, had two unique, one-of-a-kind roles: he helped establish the founding mission and vision of the church, as well as setting precedents in all areas of church life that subsequent others have followed or changed. These roles are highly important, and more so, because his historical position as the church's first pastor is significant symbolically, as well as literally.

He is the church's "founding father," if you will. As such, much like the Founding Fathers here in our country, he set the course for the direction the church now follows. It will be essential to discover this direction, as best you can, including the mission and vision God gave him at the start of the church. My own theology informs me that God brings each church into existence for a specific reason(s) that it can best accomplish, unique to that which God has created it to be. This includes its "personality" and its "style." God reveals to the embryonic church His specific vision for them and focuses them on a special audience of people who need to be reached. This is how God shapes all new churches, not simply to survive in this world, but to thrive.

> **It is crucial to ascertain "the framer's intent." In other words, why did God bring this church into existence?**

Because of the critical nature of these components, it is crucial to ascertain, as we might say today, "the framer's intent." In other words, why did God bring this church into existence? How has it fulfilled that purpose? What still needs to be done?

Remember, God never wastes an experience, so even if the church has taken a different direction or discovered a new emphasis, its identity has not changed…it has only matured. The church's future, in almost every instance, will build upon its past.

We will return as well to the impact of precedent in the next chapter. For now, it is best for us simply to remember that over time precedents tend to become traditions. Precedents are set in the life of a people for a reason; they do not appear in a vacuum. Understanding these reasons will help you make sense of the local church's culture and traditions, even when people within the church are uninformed about their origin.

Because founding pastors and their ministry carry such significant influence on the life of a church, leadership must learn all it can about this time in the life of the church. Interviews become the best tool in this process. If the founding pastor is still alive and accessible, communicate with him. Learn from him about the founding vision of the church and his experiences while there. Discover why he did what he did at the church. In addition, informally interview any charter members who may still be around and able to add their observations and feelings about that period in the church's history. Finally, it would be wise to make an appointment with any community official (including neighboring pastors) who might be able to supplement the knowledge about the founding of the church. Perceptions and opinions from these people are as important as facts, so don't discount the statements made simply because they come from outsiders. Record their views and file them away for now.

In my denominational tribe we annually file a statistical report with our national office. This "Annual Church Profile" is accessible to local churches and can be used to note patterns and trends in the life of the church over the past years, and even decades.[32] This is an additional tool that can inform leaders of significant moments in the history of the church that need to be studied, analyzed, and understood.

GROWING UP

Apparently it was Bob Dale, in his classic book *To Dream Again*, who helped readers to realize churches have a lifecycle, too.[33] In essence, Dale suggests that churches—as living organisms—experience life in ways similar to other created things. One day they are "born" and eventually, unless Jesus returns first, they will "die." In between, they move through various predictable cycles. In the early years of life, they move through the birth, growth, and what Dale calls, the structure (an organizational phase that grows out of its self-identity, preparing and equipping the church to function more efficiently), stages. This typically lasts about fifteen years.

At the zenith of its maturity the church serves effectively for an indefinite period of God's choosing, influenced by many variable factors. Often it does not continue to grow numerically, but it is still making an impact even beyond itself.

At some point, the church begins to show signs of decline. This too moves through predictable stages of nostalgia, polarization and eventually, death. At each stage the church gets progressively worse, but at every level the church can prolong its lifecycle if it is willing to do whatever is necessary. The greater the decline in the church's life, the more urgent and dramatic the effort has to be.

This book is written specifically for churches in decline and find themselves in the nostalgia stage, or moving toward polarization. It is not written for those who are in the near death stage, where a much more radical experience of "replant," akin to resurrection, must happen for the church to continue to minister effectively into the future.[34]

It is important for the leaders of the church to realize where they are in this lifecycle. For most, it will be an eye-opening experience. At first, many leaders will be in denial. They will argue that things are better than they truly are. However, the evidence uncovered, along with peers who see more clearly, will eventually ground them in reality. Remember, they must acknowledge reality before they will accept the need to change. Change is necessary for the church to move forward.

The good news is at each stage of the decline side of the church lifecycle the situation can be reversed and moved back into a growth mode. For churches in nostalgia, revitalization needs to take place. In this instance, revitalization means "fueling the fire of life within the church for the future." For churches in polarization, a more significant process of "refocusing" is needed. This term, popularized through a process with the same name, is a two-year journey of rediscovery and centering the church on its identity and purpose.[35] For churches at the point of death, we have already recommended replanting as the means to return to healthy priorities and growth.

Knowledge is power. And it is revealing. However, knowledge in and of itself, is never enough. The will to act on the reality uncovered will make or break the future of the declining church. Commitment and dedication are at the heart of any effective forward movement. Sacrifice will be inevitable. Personal preferences will need to be put aside. Comfort will have to give way for the greater good of God's glory. For this to happen, one needs to understand how the church ended up in this decline conundrum. It is a surprising realization for churches to grasp.

WHAT GOES UP MUST COME DOWN?

A few years ago, Jim Collins wrote a monograph in the business sector entitled *How the Mighty Fall*. It was, in essence, a sequel to his previous book *Good to Great*, which chronicled the experiences of eleven solid, dependable American companies that had consistently grown over the past fifteen years. In the earlier book, Collins had lauded these companies for their tireless commitment, their unyielding focus to the mission, and several other characteristics that he suggested to the readers might enable their companies to grow, too.[36] Unfortunately, he published his subsequent book because a couple of these companies had collapsed in the meantime. He attempted to explain why.

Collins suggested that as a company grows, it feeds off of its own success and this catapults it forward. In a sense this is good, for it helps the company to take risks and dare to live out the dream. But it has a dark side, too. The author suggests that such companies, if not grounded in humility, develop hubris that blinds them to the danger of what is ahead. They are deceived into believing they have a kind of invincibility that nothing can penetrate or overcome. Collins suggests they are gravely wrong in their assessment. In fact, he goes so far as to say it is this very sense of invincibility that makes their downfall inevitable and often, highly dramatic.[37]

As the church moves through its lifecycle, its growth can plant the seeds of its eventual decline.

The application for churches should be obvious: as the church moves through its lifecycle, its growth can plant the seeds of its eventual decline. Risk, borne out of pride and a sense "we can do nothing wrong" rather than dependence on God, is reckless and does long-term damage to the continued development of the church. On the other hand, there is an alternative reaction that is dangerous, as well. It is possible to stop taking risks and trusting God, but instead depend only on prior successes to sustain the church into the future. Either response jeopardizes the on-going growth of the church.

#renewbook

THE IMPORTANCE OF VISION

In *PLANTED: Starting Well, Growing Strong*, we noted that one of the characteristics that causes new churches to grow is an understanding of God's vision for the church plant and a focused concentration, striving to stay centered upon it.[38] This is crucial to its success for several reasons. First, if it is God's vision, then He desires to bless the effort through His Spirit to fulfill it. This supernatural dimension can't be overestimated. The eyes of our Heavenly Father are *"upon them who fear Him—those who depend on His faithful love"* (Psalm 33:18). His vision cannot become reality without His involvement. This is important, for it can help every church evaluate whether or not its vision statement (if it has one, at all) if God-given or man-made.

Second, this vision unites God's people around a common directive, revealed by Him and in turn, pointing people back to Him. It motivates and directs the service a church provides; it provides a filter to those who join the efforts of the church. It even enables leadership to evaluate these efforts to make sure their work is aiding them in accomplishing the vision. It keeps the life of the church centered and focused in the midst of so many options and alternatives.

Finally, vision looks ahead toward a "preferred future." Because it pulls people forward, it has a built-in ability to keep moving people onward. It offers little opportunity for a church to live in the past or settle for the way things are now. This is a very important realization for established churches. Many of them believe their best years are in the past. They relive these memories (or try to do so) often, some even pining for a reoccurrence of "the glory days." However, this does damage to the growth potential of the church.

There are several reasons for this. Settling for the way things were in the past diminishes God and His plans for the church in the years to come. It says, "what you've done, God, is good enough and we're content or comfortable with that." My theology, though, declares God is *"about to do something new"* (Isaiah 43:19), and this is for all churches, not just new church plants. Vision is one of God's ways of informing the church's "together with Him" future, of motivating it toward that future, and of reminding the church of its dependence upon Him.

A church without an understanding of God's corporate vision is unfocused and simply treading water. It is no wonder these churches are not growing. They won't move forward, if they don't know which way is ahead.

Lead the church to discover and implement God's vision for its future. It will challenge and excite the people; it will inform them of progress and enable them to celebrate success. It will reveal to them God's personal involvement in their corporate life together. It will remind them over and over, "God is not finished with us yet."

APPLY TO YOUR SETTING

1. What is the history of your church? Who are the pastors still influencing the congregation? What historical events, both good and bad, still have impact on the church?

2. Who do we need to interview to learn more? Inside the church? Outside the church?

3. Where are we in the lifecycle of a church? How is this affecting our corporate life and influence for Christ today? What can we do better, or different, that will move the church forward?

4. What is the founding vision of our church? What is the current vision? How does the initial vision inform our current vision?

QUESTIONS TO CONSIDER

1. Who are we? What makes us unique? Gives us our special personality and style?

2. Where are we headed?

3. Who is on this journey with us?

4. What does God want from us?

DIGGING DEEPER

Collins, Jim. **Good to Great.** New York: HarperBusiness, 2001.

Collins, Jim. **How the Mighty Fall.** Colorado Springs, CO; Jim Collins, 2009.

Dale, Robert. **To Dream Again.** Nashville, TN: Baptist Sunday School Board, 1981.

Mancini, Will. **Vision Unique.** San Francisco: Jossey-Bass, 2008.

Mills, David. **ReTurn: Restoring Churches to the Heart of God.** Carol Stream, IL: ChurchSmart Resources, 2005.

Morgan, Tony. **The Unstuck Church.** Nashville, TN: Thomas Nelson, 2017.

DEALING WITH BAGGAGE

The Board at First Church was deep into their conversation about the early stages of progress in their "ReNEW the Future" campaign. The membership had unified behind their efforts to reverse the decline of the church over the past decade. They had developed a conviction that God wanted them once again to grow, and they were determined to live out this calling for God's glory and honor, not their own. In addition, they had recently implemented an understanding of God's vision for the church, and with its adoption, this had given focus to the ministry and life of First Church.

All of this brought excitement to the Body as a whole, but to be honest, with some mixture of anxiety and trepidation. The church was moving into uncharted territory for the first time in many years. They knew on a spiritual level that dependence on God at every turn was absolutely essential. They also realized, on a human level, that the church had some "skeletons in the closet" they would have to unearth.

"Folks, we have experienced a good start in this effort to renew our church for the future. We have seen some significant building blocks put into place. But there is much more still to do. In my research, I have discovered part of what may be holding us back, instead of moving us forward, are certain experiences and decisions of the past."

"Like what, pastor?" asked Richard, a key leader and

native of the community where First Church meets.

"Great question, Richard," the pastor replied. "I was thinking of the tragic situation involving the former pastor fifteen years ago, who ran off with one of the deacon's wife. Oh, and the circumstances surrounding the suicide of our worship leader's son a few years back. Perhaps, even the circumstances surrounding the start of our church years ago and the subsequent way we created our bylaws and policies here at First Church...There are probably other things, too, we will discover as we delve deeper into our church's life together.

"Then, there are our traditions. These are valuable and have meaning to us as a congregation—at least they did when they were begun—but they may carry little or no meaning to the newcomers who visit or consider joining our church. Not only is it possible our own members don't know why we do these things anymore, but they may present obstacles for others as they ponder whether or not First Church is where they need to grow and serve God.

"And I wouldn't want us to forget the role of reputation in our community and how these experiences and decisions have impacted the way our townspeople view us. While their perceptions may or may not be accurate, they do color the way they see First Church. Since 'image' is one of the barriers unchurched people must overcome before considering a church possibility, we need to discover how we are perceived in the community, and if there are concerns, determine how to address them."

"Wow, that's a lot, Pastor," Richard responded. "I had no idea these kind of things could be holding us back. Perhaps we should get busy investigating our church culture and determining how to deal pro-actively with what we discover."

Over the past decade, American travelers who fly to their destination have wrestled with a number of additional fees. The 9/11 security fee has become a reality for all fliers on domestic flights. Assigned seats, depending on where you want to sit and when you want to secure them, can bring additional fees, too. There are many more, but none of these fees are as visible and irritating (at least for me!) as the baggage fees associated with luggage.

Almost every traveler carries luggage with them. The novice traveler usually carries too much, packing one or two suitcases to the limit. They will stuff their suitcases with all they know they will need, and more. They will consider contingencies (What if it rains? What if it's colder than expected? What other shoes will I need? And on and on...) I know; I used to be just like this myself. I was ready for every scenario in advance. However, I came to discover most of what I had imagined or considered never became a reality. My baggage, instead of assisting me in my experiences, actually did little but weigh me down.

As the airlines decided to begin penalizing passengers for "checking" their luggage, I, like many others, began to explore alternatives. I learned quickly the seasoned flier often packs only a carry-on bag, something lightweight and able to avoid the sinister baggage fees on almost every airline. This forced me to prepare better in anticipation of my trip and to pack only what was needed and had been prioritized as necessary for the trip ahead. Extraneous items, no matter how special to me personally, were left behind if they weren't going to help me with life while completing the journey. As a result, I was free to roam easily, and my baggage was not an albatross upon my adventure. And since I didn't check my luggage, it didn't cost me anything, nor was I penalized for what I did carry with me on the journey.

The more the church wants to carry into the future, the more it is anchored to the past.

Churches need to deal with their own baggage, too, as they prepare for the ReNEW adventure. They, no doubt, have many wonderful and meaningful experiences, traditions, and unique cultural distinctives they would like to carry with them on this journey to their preferred future. However, the more the church wants to carry into the future, the more it is anchored to the past. This hinders it from reaching its destination.

This is not to suggest that all experiences, traditions, or

#renewbook

cultural elements in the church's life up to the present must be jettisoned, or are of no future value. On the contrary, the future always builds on the present, and the present upon the past. In other words, the past is necessary to our current and future experience. But it should not be allowed to hold the church hostage as the people of God look ahead.

Every church, like human beings themselves, has "baggage." This baggage includes its history, its culture, and its lifestyle. These items are filled with both good and bad elements and moments.

How we deal with these matters differ in typical churches, though, if they are good baggage or bad baggage. If they are good items in our collective memory, churches have a tendency to recognize them, celebrate them, and hold these things in high esteem. In some ways, they become "sacred" to the local Body who has come to value their import and significance for the blessing it brings to their lives. However, if they are bad items in our collective experience, churches usually refuse to speak of them, sweep them under the proverbial rug, and pretend they never happened. With these matters, they become "elephants in the room" for the entire church and thus, hold power over its life, especially as it seeks to move forward.

Every church should intentionally and deliberately determine what baggage it will carry into the future. It is to this process we now turn.

PACKING FOR THE TRIP

As the church studies its history, something we suggested in the last chapter, it will uncover some of the more meaningful moments in its existence. These will include things like:

- The charter service
- Installation services
- First missions efforts, near or far
- First decisions for Christ and baptisms
- Joint services with other congregations

#renewbook

- New churches planted or parented
- Revivals or evangelistic emphases
- Concerts and pageants
- Bible conferences and educational efforts
- Ministries with significant impact
- Special times of prayer or communion
- Buildings built or bought for worship and ministry
- Staff additions with positive impact
- Corporate holiday experiences

There may be others, too. In general, these evoke positive responses from people within the congregation. As such, they often become protected experiences, which members, especially longtime members, guard with great diligence. For the people who value these moments, recognize that they evoke an emotional response. As such, they can't simply be dealt with at a cognitive level. Hearts have been affected and people are quick in these instances to protect such precious memories. In other words, they mean something personally, as well as corporately to the church as a whole.

Because people are emotional about these experiences, they will have a hard time letting go of them as they plan for the future. But sometimes they must. Some moments are time-stamped and can't be repeated with the same effectiveness. Or if they are, often it comes at the price of more energy, higher budgets, and greater manpower to recreate the experience in a changing world. These items, if the church is not careful, can move it toward nostalgia on the lifecycle of a church very quickly.

The past has power over you; if not careful, even our memories can become idols that keep our hearts from God.

If you've ever heard people say, "I miss the old days," "We've never done it that way before," or "Let's go back to the way we used to do that," then be forewarned: the past has power over you. You are not free; you are in bondage to the past, and moreover, you are inviting the chains to tie you up! If not careful, even your memories can become idols that keep your hearts from God.

As leaders, you must guide your church to determine which memories and experiences are holding the church back and which ones are worth packing in your luggage for the future. This is not an easy or quick process; it must be processed slowly and with great compassion. By and large, the congregation will follow your leadership IF you give them time AND listen to their concerns. When their heart speaks, respond with love.

In addition to these positive experiences, there are (almost always positive) traditions in the life of every church. Tradition is not a bad word, even though some younger church leaders and church planters seem to think so. Tradition is simply a habitual way of dealing with something, due to the value it brings those involved in accomplishing the concern at hand. It is built upon the precedents we discussed in the previous chapter. Here's how it works.

When needs arise, congregations led by their leadership, determine how to respond to them. This response sets precedent in the church's life within the certain situation or circumstance addressed. If the leadership and congregation is pleased with the precedent, they will repeat the process in similar situations. Over time, it becomes a tradition, or "the way we do things around here." As such, it weaves its way into the fabric of the local church's culture and way of life. Over time, these traditions become so familiar that no one questions their functionality.

In church life, traditions are not theology, but rather are based upon it. They are personalized interpretations of theology, customized to our time and space continuum. In other words, the Bible teaches us to observe the Lord's Supper. But how and when should we observe it? Churches will determine their own response to these questions, and as a result, will develop customized traditions to deal with them.

The trouble is over time these traditions are treated as much like Scripture as the Word of God itself. Like the

Pharisees of old—the masters of religious tradition—we fail to remember the difference. And this creates problems.

What are these traditions, you wonder? Unfortunately, since they are locally created and contextually owned, the possibilities are limitless. Here, though, are a few of the more common ones:

- Time and place of worship
- When and how we observe baptism
- When and how we observe the Lord's Supper
- Dress code
- The music (and instruments) in worship
- Sermon style
- Use of technology
- Decision/Response time
- Written or visual material
- How the church conducts "business"
- Additional times/reasons (beyond Sunday) the church gathers
- Annual church anniversary or celebrations
- Holiday celebrations
- Ministries we share
- When and how we teach others the Bible
- How we select lay leaders (and pastors, in many instances)
- New member process
- Outreach programs and missions efforts

The list could go on and on. There are myriad examples. Churches need to know the traditions that are "owned" by the congregation. Studying the constitution and bylaws, or other governing documents within a church, reveals many of these traditions. Outsiders or fringe attendees (those who are new to the church or not deep inside the church culture yet) can help discover others, as well. Analyze these as they surface. Ask why the tradition exists and if it is fulfilling the function intended. Then determine if its value is worth extending into the future, and act accordingly.

"UNMENTIONABLES"

When packing for a trip, there are certain things we carry with us that we rarely mention to others, or perhaps, even want them to know. It is the same with churches, too. Their baggage is not all visible and open for everyone to see; some of it remains hidden or ignored. Sometimes, this is because it embarrasses the church or causes it shame. Or it may cause the church great pain and the people have not let go of it yet. At still other times, the church may not even be aware of its presence, yet it still carries influence over their life experience. It is a heavy burden to bear for all affected.

These experiences are the dark underbelly of church life. If leaders are honest, most churches have some of these experiences over the years, just as most families have some skeletons in the closet themselves. In recent years, American society has "called out" church life in this area, bringing to light sexual scandals and financial escapades of biblical proportions, and rightly so. They have shined the light on these ugly "elephants in the room" churches refuse to face. But face them the church must.

Psychologically, Christians don't want to admit to such behavior in church life, since God's people are commanded to live holy lives. They have sinned, but they do not want to admit this to others, either. Because of this, church members mask their failings with sanctimonious verbiage and misdirection. Unfortunately, failure to admit this sinfulness indicts the church with hypocrisy and dysfunction.

We can never be well until we go to the Great Physician. We will never go to Him unless we are willing to admit our ills. We will never admit our ills until we acknowledge our need.

Compound this with the pain churches feel over the sudden death of a key leader, the abrupt departure of a pastor, a catastrophic natural disaster, or something similar. The congregation will be scarred and battered, as a result. Yet, often their "victorious" theology of overcoming leaves little room, or grants little permission, to face their hurts and grieve as they should.

Kenneth Quick, in his book *Healing the Heart of Your Church,* has addressed these concerns in great detail. It is an excellent book and well worth reading. Its insights are deep and helpful for churches that deal with experiences often swept under the rug of congregational life.[39] These include things like:

- Affairs or sexual misconduct by church leadership
- Financial misconduct
- Church splits
- Tragic death of a current leader
- Sinful reactivity (strife, bitterness, rebellion)

These concerns, and others like them, create spiritual barriers that hinder the growth and development of God's church. Though they are spiritual concerns, they are typically dealt with on a material, physical level only, if they are dealt with at all. Usually they are addressed quickly, with as little public involvement or attention as possible. They are then thrown in the closet of shameful church experience. The desire is never to deal with them again. However, unless they are handled openly and fully, these issues will resurface, usually at the most inopportune moments.

Quick outlines an extensive process based upon the Scriptures by which a church can do "surgery" on these spiritual diseases, and then heal appropriately.[40] Having gone through the process myself, I can testify to its thoroughness and its effectiveness. If the church you lead is truly serious about ridding itself of unnecessary baggage that hinders it from moving forward, I seriously recommend you deal with it on a spiritual level, as well as a physical one. God will be honored, trust within the congregation will be gained, and credibility within the community will be enhanced.

IMAGE IS EVERYTHING?

There was a Canon® camera commercial that ran a few years ago, featuring then number one male tennis star, Andre Agassi. It was promoting the "Rebel" line of cameras (appropriate for Agassi, if you remember anything about his life) and touting the slogan, spoken by the tennis star, "Image is everything." While I don't totally agree with the statement, I do understand its emphasis. How people "see" you (important to a camera company) affects both their involvement with you and their influence upon others regarding you. Image involves perception; perception addresses reputation.

Reputation is not the same as "who you truly are." The genuine nature of your identity is wrapped up in your integrity and the character that demonstrates it. Reputation, on the other hand, is who people think you are. It is what they see or hear, and what others tell them about you, influencing their beliefs and actions toward you.

Reputation is important. Churches need to realize much of what they do and say falls on deaf ears because of reputation. On the other hand, sometimes it enhances the life of a church. It impacts the church both ways. It has been said that after a positive experience with a church, a person will tell one or two people; but if a person has a bad experience with a church, they will inform three or more persons. For many people, this is how a church's reputation becomes known to them.

Church plants almost never have a negative reputation in the community when they start. They usually don't have a positive one, either. They fight a different battle—the battle of ignorance. People in the community don't even know they exist. They rarely have a building with their name on it. They have few, if any, members at the start. As a result, they have to create a reputation from scratch. This is done through positive pubic relations efforts and word-of-mouth marketing, for the most part. And it works!

Established churches have two varied reputations in their own community: either they are known as a people who care about the community and where God is at work, or they are considered a critic of the community with baggage they refuse to acknowledge, making them "hypocrites" in the minds of outsiders. While overly simplistic, readers hopefully can see the significant difference reputation can make in reaching others for Jesus. Churches who don't care about their reputation have contributed to a barrier the unchurched must traverse, if they are ever to be reached with the Gospel. Moreover, they fail to recognize that if they handle their own reputation poorly, it has a ripple effect upon other churches, starting with those closest to them in tribe and geography.

Established churches can re-create their reputation, if desired. It starts with the heart; a church must be willing to confront the things hindering its image within the community at large. They do this in three ways. First, church leadership needs to get out into the community and be visible in ministry. This initiative starts best by finding one or two ways they can help town leaders make the community a better place to live and experience life to its fullest. Interviews with community leaders, including but not limited to the mayor, city manager, councilpersons, police chief, fire chief, and school superintendent, will provide a wealth of information about needs and possible ways the church can be of assistance. Church leaders need to find the most effective way they can participate, based on the filters of their theology (nothing compromises the Gospel) and their giftedness (whom God has brought into the church). Positive influence through action rather than words starts turning the tide of public opinion.

Second, established churches need to be brutally honest and transparent regarding their past failings. They must admit to being a "hospital for sinners," not a "clubhouse for only saints." They must acknowledge their shortcomings and weaknesses and admit to needing Jesus as much as anyone else. The church must identify with the community on a human level, not as its accuser or judge, but rather as its friend and advocate. They must cause others to see them not as promoting a "better than thou" attitude, but a "by this they will know" attitude. They must love others as they love themselves.

Third, any marketing or public relations strategy deployed should start with the above two items. Demonstrate that actions speak louder than words. Be open and honest with community officials and the townspeople about the shortcomings of the past. Then and only then, add an additional public relations strategy built primarily on word-of-mouth experience. Find those church members and new attendees known among the unchurched who can be encouraged to consider the church. It could go something like this: "You've been blessed to be a part of this church. Whom do you know needing to experience this same kind of blessing in their life, too?" Motivate the membership to tell others what God is doing in the midst of the church. Save any tangible marketing until after the tide of public opinion has turned favorable again for the church.

CONSTRAINING STRUCTURE

In *PLANTED*, I write that limiting the infrastructure of the church frees it to grow quickly, without encumbrance.[41] Too often the structures of a church are confining, choking the life right out of the church. Duty calls our name, but joy is missing in the job. It saps the church of vitality, making service a chore rather than a celebration. It restricts participation rather than blessing involvement, because structure requires opportunity to "fit our mold."

In effective church plants, this is not the case. They have limited structure, believing "less is more." Less structure allows for greater freedom, more flexibility, and quicker response to opportunities. It builds relational trust, promotes the Holy Spirit's leadership in the life of the church, and gives permission for leadership to bless others with innovation in ministry. It holds tightly to *"sola Scriptura,"* and treats the Body with dignity and value as family members for who they are, not simply what they do.

Not all established churches are different from this, to be sure. However, many are, though they did not start that way. Here's why. Initial structure (constitution and bylaws, policies and procedures, organizational charts, and decision-making processes) took place informally through consensus and relationships. Somewhere in the growth experience of the lifecycle of the church, leadership recognized a need for a more formal way to deal with some or all of these items. A constitution and bylaws were hammered out and adopted. These were likely developed from one of several sources: a template containing generic elements often found in a church's structure, a favorite church or ministry that influenced the church planter or pastor who started the church, or as a reaction to another church (where the planter came from, others in town, etc.).

These documents rightly spell out the boundaries for church life and its legal status in the eyes of the government. They share a statement of faith and membership requirements. They speak of officers and often indicate the church's purpose and even its potential dissolution. Often, though, they go beyond these elements to speak of programming (including business meetings!) and scheduling issues, as well. These aspects are more rightly recognized as methodological preferences than identity elements.

Over time these governing documents change. Human nature suggests they tend to enlarge, not shrink, because we have a tendency to think of new things we want included and add them, rather than removing things that are awkward, cumbersome, or not applicable. These additions are of two types: something we find elsewhere we like and want incorporated into the life of the church, or more likely, a reaction to something that has gone wrong in church life. These gaps or inadequacies are filled in with new restrictions and procedures to make sure this "wrong" doesn't happen again, or if it does, that the church deals with it in a more appropriate way. While the intent is often well-meaning, the result binds the church in a more restrictive way.

> **Too little structure may leave the church unfocused; too much structure squeezes the life right out of the church.**

Add to this the reality in most churches that a few persons enjoy politics and business more than Scripture and ministry, and it is a potentially volatile mixture ready to explode. When opportunities come along, these individuals are the ones who will typically pull out the documentation of the church, in order to restrict the Body from moving forward rather than to bless it. The objective is control, and the result is that everybody else—including most importantly, those outside the church and without Jesus—loses.

According to Bob Dale's lifecycle thesis, growth tends to plateau and later, decline after a focused period of organization and structure.[42] These elements have the ability to give form and shape to the life of the church, and to channel life together efficiently. But this is more an art than a science. Too little structure may leave the church unfocused. But too much structure squeezes the life right out of the church. I personally would opt for less, not more, every time.

For a church to grow again, it needs to streamline the organizational processes and maximize the ministry opportunities that surface. This means leadership in the church will need to revisit these documents and procedures to assess whether or not they are enhancing ministry for the church, or hindering it. In doing so, select a handful of people to review these documents together, and have them ask the following questions in their review:

- How does this impact our ability to respond quickly and appropriately where we see God at work?
- Is this time-dated or does it suggest a methodology rather than an objective we need to accomplish?
- Does this bless people and give them permission to use their giftedness or does it restrict them to do only what we want them to do?
- Does this help us accomplish our purpose and God's current vision for this church?
- Is this reactive in nature and really necessary for the Body as a whole?
- Are we depending on this more than, or as a substitute for, the Holy Spirit?

These questions are a good starting point. Others will surface as the process progresses. Seek to make the documents life-giving, affirming, and a celebration of life together as the family of God. This perspective will change a lot in the life of the church. Granted, leaders will probably wrestle with a few key people who want more rules and regulations in place. These individuals will disapprove of reviewing, and subsequently removing, some of these elements. This is human nature once again at work. At its worst, it is suspicious and thinks the worst of others. However, for the future of the church, God's people must overcome these impulses, and the desire for control, by submitting to the Spirit's redemptive leadership in lives and the church as a whole.

This takes the right kind of leadership from the pastor and those others serving the congregation, as well. It is to this role that we now turn our attention.

APPLY TO YOUR SETTING

1. What are the memories and experiences of our church that are worth keeping? Why? What value do they represent or give to us as God's people?

2. How do we handle traditions in our church life? Why do we have them? Should we keep them? Why?

3. What are the "unmentionables" in our church's history? Have we dealt with them appropriately? What do we still need to do in dealing with them?

4. Have we reviewed our governing documents lately? What do they say about us as a people? How are they life-giving, affirming, and celebratory?

5. Are we aware of our reputation as a church within our community? How are we addressing this?

QUESTIONS TO CONSIDER

1. What is the value of tradition for us?

2. Of what corporate sins do we need to repent?

3. What do our governing documents say about us as God's people, and our relationship with him and each other?

4. When people hear of our church, what is the first thing that comes to their mind?

DIGGING DEEPER

Blanchard, Bill. **Church Structure that Works.** Sisters, OR: VMI Publishers, 2008.

Dean, Justin. **PR Matters: A Survival Guide for Church Communicators.** Atlanta: DOXA Media Group, 2017.

MacDonald, Mark. **Be Known for Something.** Houston: High Bridge Books, 2017.

Miller, Donald. **Building a StoryBrand.** New York: HarperCollins Leadership, 2017.

Quick, Kenneth. **Healing the Heart of the Church.** Carol Stream, IL: ChurchSmart Resources, 2003.

Stanley, Andy. **Deep and Wide.** Grand Rapids, MI: Zondervan, 2016.

TOUR GUIDE

Pastor Stephen was struggling. To be sure, the efforts at change had met with some success. Internally, the church had taken up the task of reviewing its structure and streamlining it for greater effectiveness. In addition, they had jettisoned some of the baggage from the past as they dealt with it more appropriately. They had even found the community more receptive and accepting of them as they reached out to engage it.

Still, this had been hard for Pastor Stephen. He had seen some people leave the church over the changes made and the shift in focus to reaching those without Christ. And he had used his influence and credibility to move the church toward this process and away from the "business as usual" approach First Church had followed for many years. As a result, he felt more vulnerable than he had in years; he wondered how much more the Body would accept from his leadership before they indicated, "This is enough."

He was in uncharted territory. He had never led an effort like this. So, while he knew that in some ways what he was doing was similar to that of a church planter in his first church, he also knew that his situation was different. It was more complex. As such, it needed more prayer, more patience, more wisdom, and more perseverance.

Pastor Stephen was thankful he had Pastor Joe's encouragement in the process. He knew having his wife to support and encourage him was important, but it wasn't enough. Yet, he knew Pastor Joe did not fully understand his dilemma, either. He was grateful his longtime friend and mentor, Pastor Bill could advise him, as well. Pastor Bill was retired now, but had been a supporter and confidante down through the years of ministry. He had seen many things and had shared a great deal of wisdom with Stephen and others over the years.

"Stay the course, Stephen," Pastor Bill reminded him. "God called you to this journey, so don't back away.

"There may be scars you receive along the way, but as long as they are not fatal, they won't kill you. Rather, they define you. They give evidence to the unique way God is shaping and using you, just as He did the apostle Paul many years ago.

"Here in the middle of the journey, what the church needs most is a steady hand, a captain with confidence in his Maker, who will guide you safely to the shore. You need to be that captain: a calm, confident presence who plots and navigates his journey by the heavens.

"Have faith in God. And be the leader God created you to be. Remember, you are not alone in this adventure. Let God direct you each step of the way. He knows what He's doing; do you?"

My wife, Joyce, and I have enjoyed traveling abroad several times over the thirty-two years of our marriage. The journeys have been amazing! Our favorite destination is Europe; we have been to England, France, Germany, Switzerland, the Netherlands, and Italy, among others. Our most memorable visit ever was to Venice, Italy, on our 25th wedding anniversary trip. This city, built upon 118 islands surrounded by water and invaded with canals, takes local transportation to an entirely new level. Taxis are far more frequent on the water than on the ground. Everywhere you walk, you cross bridges and see boats or gondolas. The moments they create are memorable and spectacular.

As is our custom when visiting new places where we have never previously been, we join a tour group, in hopes of better understanding and appreciating the history and culture of what we see around us. Tour groups, like the one we joined in Venice, are no different; a tour guide, who knows his or her way around, leads these groups. Our guide, Sophia, took us to St. Mark's Basilica, the Piazza San Marco nearby, and the Fortress of the Doges, who ruled Venice for many years. We explored the streets, heard the stories, and visited the canals. It was an experience Joyce and I will never forget!

The pastor of the established church on the quest toward God's destination serves as the tour guide for your revitalization journey. While you may not know the end point of the adventure and what it will look like, you know the Owner, and He leads you every step of the way. In addition, the key leaders will assist the pastor on this adventure. However, it all starts with the pastor, so here then, is where we begin.

KNOW YOURSELF

If you are a pastor and find yourself reading this book, you likely fall into one of two categories: a former church planter now pastoring, or one who has never planted a church at all. If you fall into the first category, I have some good news for you: draw on the planting skills you used in those days to guide your leadership now in this current church. In addition to what I mention in chapter one of this book, you will find a significant chapter in my previous book, *PLANTED: Starting Well, Growing Strong*, that emphasizes the role you play in directing the efforts of the current church to renew the vitality and growth God desires.[43]

For those of you who have never been a church planter, the objective is to "think and act" as much like a church planter in this current situation as you can, and at the same time, continue to be yourself. So, how does a church planter think and act? How is that different from a typical pastor?

These are important questions and will help you evaluate yourself, to find how similar your shaping from God may be to that of effective church planters. Charles Ridley, Professor of Counseling Psychology at Indiana University, formulated an assessment tool many years ago to help interviewers assess candidates for church planting. It has become the cornerstone for measuring the potential of church planting candidates. His research found thirteen characteristics stood out among all effective North American church planters, regardless of age or ethnicity. They are:

- Visioning Capacity
- Intrinsically Motivated
- Creates Group Ownership
- Passion for the Lost and Unchurched
- Spousal Cooperation
- Effectively Builds Relationships
- Responsive to the Community
- Builds Group Cohesiveness
- Committed to Church Growth
- Utilizes the Giftedness of Others
- Resilient
- Flexible and Adaptable
- Extraordinary Faith[44]

These characteristics form the foundation of an effective church planter. A few of them stand out and may be critical to your ability to think and act like a church planter. These include visioning capacity, a passion for the lost and unchurched, effectively builds relationships, responsive to the community, committed to church growth, and flexible and adaptable. Are you strong in these areas? If not, can you surround yourself with others who are and then, empower them to use their strengths effectively?

Are you strong in these areas? If not, can you surround yourself with others who are, and then empower them to use their strengths effectively?

However, there are other elements in the makeup of a church planter that differ from pastors, too. I have written about this previously in an unpublished work. They include:

- Motivation – vision, not operation
- Role – catalytic leader, not a care-giving nurturer

- Focus – simple and centered, not broad and varied
- Personality type – typically thinkers, not feelers...and extraverts, not introverts
- Orientation – lives in the future, not the present or the past

So, how do you measure up? Remember, the goal here is not to turn you into a church planter, but to tap into abilities, surfaced or latent, that will enable you to lead your church forward in growth, as effective church planters do.

Regardless of your experience in the church planting world previously, your role as leader of this journey will depend upon your confidence in God's calling, and your determination and focus in keeping the congregation together as you head to the destination. It relies on your leadership skills in moving the church forward until they arrive safely at the end of the journey.

Your confidence in God's calling is crucial to those following you.[45] They need to know from you that this destination, and the subsequent direction, is what God is challenging them to do. They need a sense you are not simply following a formula, or even the suggestions of a book like this, more than you are waiting before the Lord and learning from Him what needs to be done. They are right. This reality must be true in your life.

Your work as the undershepherd of this flock needs to be undergirded in much prayer. Leadership requires wisdom and discernment; some of this is discovered through the gauntlets of experience. Still more, though, demands you stay before the Father, and listen to Him. The Scripture reminds us, *"If any of you lacks wisdom, he should ask God—who gives to all generously and ungrudgingly"* (James 1:5). Wisdom will lead to confidence, and confidence will strengthen your leadership.

Don't forget, though, that there will always be what Henry Blackaby calls "the crisis of unbelief."[46] God will stretch you, too, as a leader, to trust Him more, for there will be twists and turns on this journey you will be unable to anticipate or predict. In those moments, you must demonstrate your confidence is grounded upon faith in God and His ample provision. This confidence calms the fears of the congregation and strengthens your leadership among them. So, "don't be afraid; only believe."

Second, you as leader on this journey must keep everyone focused clearly on the objective of this renewal growth initiative. There will be plenty of potential distractions along the way, and you must not let the congregation drift. This takes resolute determination and unfettered concentration on the destination. Moreover –and this may be the most important thing you can bring to the table as the pastor and leader – you MUST build momentum toward the objective in mind.

How do you do that? I have addressed this at some length in chapter three of this book. In *PLANTED*, I also suggested you as leader function as "cheerleader" for your congregants.[47] You must encourage, equip, and empower them to be active participants in the process. As pastor, you must support them and "have their back." Complimenting them, affirming them, and appreciating them will add fire to their own motivation to get involved. You must find appropriate ways to do this—appropriate both to who you are and to who they are (for everybody is different, thus, there is no standard way to do this for all).

Finally, your own leadership skills must be honed and strengthened for the journey. Whenever leaders truly lead, there are a few (usually vocal) dissenters. Many pastors are "people pleasers," and as such, they desire not to offend anyone. The result can be little or no forward movement in the growth and development of the congregation. A few persons can hold hostage the future possibilities of the church. This should not be; eternal lives are at stake and often hang in the balance.

Pastor, if God has called you to this, expect the Devil to find ways to oppose you! Refuse to compromise or give in; deal compassionately but firmly with those who attempt to stop the church's effort. Remember you ultimately serve only an audience of One. If He has called you to this, He will sustain you through it.

LONGEVITY HAS ITS BENEFITS

Researchers have discovered pastors who have served at their current church seven years or more have much more significant impact on the church than those who serve shorter tenures.[48] For one thing, they usually have brought a majority of the congregation into the church during their tenure. Their credibility and influence at this point tends to carry more weight than any of their predecessors who served as pastor (of course, some exceptions apply). In addition, they tend to "reap the benefits" of their longevity among the congregation. The congregation now sees the pastor as "one of us," not an outsider, whose leadership and ideas can be trusted and followed.

This is important, because established churches with pastors of seven plus years of service will likely face minimal opposition to a forward-thinking growth initiative like this. While they may surprise some members or find some pushback from those who have been with them through the years (especially if they haven't lobbied for this kind of emphasis in the past), few long-tenured pastors face enough opposition to derail the process. Here is where the courage of the pastor and the certainty of God's call strengthen him to lead the people ahead. *"For such a time as this"* (Esther 4:14) may truly apply to these pastors in established churches.

On the other hand, if you are a newer pastor with shorter years of service in an established church, the chances are higher that you will meet opposition and resistance to an initiative like this, especially if the church anticipates it will cost a great deal of time and money. This is also true if other programs or initiatives are jeopardized as a result of this new growth effort. Recognize you may not have enough clout and credibility with the congregation to gain support for this kind of effort—yet.

RALLYING THE TROOPS

Above all, your leadership must sound the trumpet of God's vision for His people in the church. This must be the unifying factor, engaging their hearts and inspiring their minds. It must challenge them to sacrifice personal amenities, like comfort and convenience, for eternal gain. Make sure everyone knows and understands this is not about you and its not your agenda; this is for God and it is His agenda you seek to fulfill. Keep the focus on Him at all times.

In doing that, rejoice with the people when the church meets some of its goals and experiences successes, no matter how small. These small steps forward motivate people to do more and will enhance the unity they experience. It will help them realize they are making a difference in the world, especially the world that matters most to them, the world that is their own. It disarms dissenters, silencing them as a result of its success.

Share these successes in narrative, story form whenever possible. People tend to respond better to story forms than other means of communication today. So, find ways to have people tell the church, or groups within the church, of their own experience. This can be done through testimonies (live or video), interviews, letters that are written to the church Body as a whole, or within a column of your newsletter. These stories carry impact, are remembered for a long time, and have additional peripheral value for the effort, as well. Add to these stories meaningful times of prayer for those involved, both servants and those saved, and it will fuel the congregation forward in an even greater way.

Remember, vision engages people at a heart level.

Remember, vision engages people at a heart level. So, address it in artistic form, too, through photographs, music, and other means that your church may be gifted to use. Even baptism and the Lord's Supper can remind people of God's revealed vision for the congregation. And if done well, this vision is personalized, and it has its own way of speaking into the heart of an individual and pulling them forward toward its eventual fulfillment. The vision points them to their Savior.

EMPOWERING OTHERS

As the pastor, you have a lot riding on the outcome of this effort. The desire is to reverse a declining trend, to refocus people on God and His love for the lost still around you. You have likely sacrificed, taken on a few new scars, and experienced some pushback along the way. So, in many ways it is understandable that you want to hold tight to the reins of this process. You are the Guide for the church, after all.

These thoughts are justifiable and are correct on so many levels. It is usually true that no one has more at stake in this process than the pastor himself. However, one possible consequence of this attitude is a desire to control the process and possibly, even its results. And that would be a mistake, for several reasons.

On a very significant level, people have to own decisions like this themselves. This cannot be a surrogate experience; it needs to be personal. It must become a part of who they are as a people and what they want to see happen. If the pastor holds on too highly, others cannot take ownership...or refuse to do so. If this is their experience, then they will usually not participate (at least, not for long) or get involved. And consequently, the pastor is the one who stands to carry the blame if it does not work out as expected.

Another reason this is problematic is it minimizes the giftedness and role of the people within the Body. Ephesians 4:11-12 suggests leaders are to equip the people for works of service. To do this sufficiently, people must not only learn about their giftedness, but be blessed to use this giftedness appropriately. Since Christ is the Head of the Body, this is a good reminder that the church and its growth effort are not about the pastor; rather, this is all about God.

Everyone needs to remember the pastor will not be in his role forever; someone will eventually replace him (unless Jesus returns first). Because this is true, the church needs to own this initiative, not simply the pastor.

Finally, here's a pragmatic reason: the pastor can't do it all alone. He is a limited, finite person, who can only touch so many others, and handle so many responsibilities himself. In fact, God created the church is such a way that certain people will respond better if they are connected or reached by persons other than the pastor, anyway. We all need each other. Every part within the Body of Christ is important, valued, and needs to do its part.

Remember: if you are the pastor, then you will most often attract other people like yourself. And this is likely not the only ones you hope the church is able to reach with the Gospel. Others need to be reached, too, who are different from you. But this only happens, when you are equipping and empowering the congregation to attract or reach others, too.

It takes all kinds of people to reach all kinds of people.

No one can do it alone. No matter how great a leader you are, you by yourself are not enough to reach everyone God wants reached. So, guide people to their role on this marvelous adventure. Ensure they have what they need to be successful. Remind them they are not alone in their service. Give them the freedom to own their part of this journey.

Then, be their biggest fan and advocate. Pray for them continually. Check on them regularly. Troubleshoot obstacles for them, as needed. And celebrate with them when the victories take place.

This is what leaders do.
This is what you must do.
Be the leader God wants you to be.

To be that leader, you will have to lead the church to make some tough calls. Many of these will be in regards to prioritizing items in the budget and calendar, as it pertains to the future. The revitalization of the church will depend to some degree on the decisions made here. So, it is to these needs that we turn our attention next.

APPLY TO YOUR SETTING

1. How is our pastor like a church planter? Different from a church planter? What difference will that potentially make in our revitalization effort?

2. How long has our pastor been serving with us? Does he currently have enough credibility and trust earned to lead us through this process?

3. Who can our pastor rely on to support him in his role? How can he empower them to work with him to accomplish more in this process than any one person can ever do?

4. Whose stories need to be told to add momentum to this effort? How is it best to share them?

QUESTIONS TO CONSIDER

1. What can we celebrate? How will we celebrate it?

2. What can we do to build credibility and trust among the congregation?

3. Who already owns the vision in our church? Who else needs to own it?

4. Is this the right time to move forward? Are the right people in place?

DIGGING DEEPER

Blackaby, Henry T. and King, Claude V. **Experiencing God.** Nashville, TN: LifeWay Christian Resources, 1990.

Jackson, J. David. **Elevate! Growing Your New Church, Years 3-7**, revised (unpublished), 2017.

Malphurs, Aubrey. **Leading Leaders.** Grand Rapids, MI: Baker Books, 2005.

Maxwell, John. **The Leadership Handbook.** Nashville, TN: Thomas Nelson, 2008.

Ridley, Charles R. and Logan, Robert E. with Helena Gerstenberg. **Training for Selection Interviewing.** Carol Stream, IL: ChurchSmart Resources, 1998.

7

RESOURCING THE JOURNEY

Pastor Stephen was thankful his congregation was supportive of his ministry. He heard horror stories from other pastors regarding the way they struggled in leadership with their members. He was grateful God provided a family of faith who had loved and supported him over the years at First Church, and now were stepping up to the plate to do their part in this new effort to move forward as a church. They had slowly come on board as he reported the victories won and the lives changed. Hearing the stories excited the people! They rejoiced in God's work among them again.

As vitality and enthusiasm returned to the church family, more and more people wanted to get involved. Pastor Stephen learned quickly that he didn't have the time or ability to keep up with all God was doing, so he trained and equipped everyone who was willing to play a part in this ongoing drama. In addition, he kept them focused on the destination – God's revealed vision – and cheered them on from a distance, as well as face-to-face.

He knew he needed to do more, though. "Any leader who truly cares about those joining the adventure needs to resource them effectively." At the beginning of this process, there was little need for many expenditures, or even scheduling issues to be addressed. Members and attendees were encouraged to build interest personally, through investment of personal time in their regular world of relationships. This word-of-mouth impact didn't cost the church much, though it did have to clear some of its calendared items for the members to spend more time engaging their personal worlds with the Gospel.

"Now we have come to the place where we have to look harder at our scheduling, to see how we're asking our members to use their time and energy," Pastor Stephen thought. "We can't keep adding activity to their already-busy lives; we must prioritize and make sure we are 'redeeming the time,' as the apostle Paul states it.

"And we must also look at the budget, too. The same prioritization has to take place there. We need to invest more of the funds God is bringing us for His heart's desire that others come to know Him as Savior and Lord.

"As a church, it is time for us to begin some corporate efforts to impact the community together. This will take us out among the people, and it will show them the powerful witness of a united community of faith, serving in Christ's love, for their sake and those they know and love."

Annually, since very early in our marriage, my wife Joyce has insisted we plan for a week of vacation. Early on, I believe she realized if I didn't calendar it, then it wasn't going to happen. I fill my schedule up with an overwhelming number of other things to do, all of them good and at least in my opinion, important. And to be honest, she is right about this. I am a "doer" by nature, so I am always adding more and more to my calendar and rarely, subtracting anything at all.

I suppose a psychologist would have a field day with me on this matter (other matters, too, I suspect): she or he might declare I am finding my personal worth in my activity, or I consider myself irreplaceable. And she or he would likely be right; I've been programmed to believe my importance—at least part of it—is in doing much.

Joyce has taught me, though, that this belief is not accurate. My worth is not in doing much, but in doing right. What she means by this is one's worth is not found in how busy you are, or how much you do, but rather, in the prioritizing of what's important in life. Jesus reminded us, *"One's life is not in the abundance of his possessions"* (Luke

12:15b). While Jesus' words are often taken to refer simply to money and possessions, perhaps it does us all well to recognize that time is one of the commodities we all have in our possession, as well. How we use it says a lot about us.

Vacation says family is important and rest is needed. These values and experiences deserve to be priorities in life. Because they are important, time must be carved out of an already complex schedule for them to take place. Otherwise, additional unintended concerns (health, for example) and complexities (other work opportunities) may arise that compromise the integrity of these needed values. Priorities order complexity. Simplicity supplies strength.

Obviously, scheduling these priorities is not enough. Joyce and I have to budget funds for a vacation to take place. Whether we streamline it and stay at home, or travel as a guest somewhere because of a friend's hospitality, or take a trip to some exotic location that is far away from anything or anyone we know, it still incurs expenses. Money is necessary to support the values we hold dear.

I was reminded this week to cherish the moments we have; you never know when they won't be available anymore. In tough times, we clarify our experiences and our values surface. What really matters rises to the top.

Churches are this way, too. We plan a great deal of activity and we resource accordingly. But what does our activity and our funding say about what is really important to us? And beyond that, how does it match up with what is really important to our Heavenly Father?

Excellent stewardship of what God puts in our care – including our time and financial resources – require us to appropriate our efforts according to God's agenda and not our own. It demands we know why we do what we do, and the certainty that our response pleases the Father.

So, let me speak frankly about this most delicate of matters: if the church is going to move forward, it is going to require time and money be appropriated adequately for the efforts at hand. If not, then such a church's priorities are telling, indeed. Jesus said, *"Where your treasure is, there your heart will be also"* (Matthew 6:21). If God wants *"all to come to repentance"* (2 Peter 3:9), if He *"loved the world in this way: He gave His one and only Son"* (John 3:16) and if He has commissioned us to *"go, therefore, and make disciples of all nations (ta ethne, from which we get the word 'ethnicities')"* (Matthew 28:19), then it stands to reason He wants us to adjust our calendars and budgets for others, beyond ourselves.

Unfortunately, even the most well-intentioned of churches, who are eager to adopt much of what they read here, may have difficulties adjusting. Many funds are fixed expenses and as a result, are virtually impossible to change. Most calendars leave little room to maneuver. So, where do we begin?

IT ALL STARTS WITH THE HEART

The answer is easy. If we desire to have long term impact, and not see this simply as a quick fix or a novel idea, then it must be addressed at the heart level. Members in the church must begin to see the world around them as God sees it. And as leaders we must constantly keep this before them. Why must we hound them with continual reminders that "lost people matter to God" and that "the church exists for others?" Well, the Scripture says it is because *"the heart is more deceitful than anything else, and incurable..."* (Jeremiah 17:9). Left to our own devices over time, human beings tend to make almost everything about themselves.

If it matters to God, it has to matter to His people. If not, they are only playing church, not being the church.

Not all churches, and the members of which they are a part, desire to grow. They know growth will bring change. It may create discomfort. It will certainly stretch the status quo. And this does not appeal to many people who are already within a church. They are fine with the way life in the congregation is currently lived.

Followers of Christ must rise above this tendency. And they must plan accordingly. If it matters to God, it has to matter to His people. If not, they are only playing church, not being the church.

Obviously, it will mean sacrifice, a word twenty-first century Americans do not like, at all. However, it is a biblical value, embraced by Jesus (Hebrews 10:12) and taught by the apostles to subsequent followers of Christ (1 Peter 2:5). It has intrinsic advantages for disciples, too. For one thing, it helps to clarify values and priorities, reminding them what is important and of lasting, eternal significance. It also keeps believers dependent upon God, since sacrifice demonstrates willingness to trust God for personal needs, even as followers place the concerns of others above their own. Finally, followers identify with their Master, who sacrificed His own life on their behalf.

When it comes to depending on God for the provision needed to serve Him, little is more telling in a church's life than this. If the church is operating simply like a business, it will look at profit-loss margins, cost effectiveness, and balance sheets. But if it is living together as a family instead, it will make the sacrifices necessary and will adjust its own needs accordingly. It is a matter of the heart.

STATUS QUO = DISOBEDIENCE

These thoughts above need to be more than simply personal opinion. They must rest on Scripture for them to demand our obedience.

- The church is God's idea, not that of any human being (Matthew 16:18).
- The Head of the church is Jesus, not any human being (Ephesians 1:22).
- As founder and Head of the church, our Lord gets to set the agenda (Matthew 28:19-20; Acts 1:8).
- Humans become a part of the church solely because of what Christ has done for us on the Cross (Ephesians 2:13).
- Our responsibility and privilege is to obey Him and follow His leadership (Acts 5:29).
- Obedience is an act of love (John 14:15).

JOB ONE

Ford Motor Company had a commercial on network television in the 1990s that proclaimed, "Quality is job one." By this they meant to suggest their top priority was to make a top-notch product upon which you could depend, one others would consider excellent in its field. While readers may debate whether or not they achieved their priority, Ford still prioritized quality, because they knew its value, if held deeply, would determine their behavior.

What is the church's "job one?" How would your church answer this question?

Some people argue that the church's top priority is worship. They suggest that ultimately our number one reason for existence is "to glorify God, and to enjoy Him forever." I would agree with this statement. However, I would not agree with the interpretation of some regarding the word "glorify." Those who mean to suggest the word equates "worship" as a distinct, compartmentalized way of praising God, separate from say, discipleship or evangelism, or from an entire lifestyle found in devoted followers of Christ, would encounter my passionate disagreement. We glorify God in the entirety of our lives, not simply on Sunday mornings.

Others would argue the church's top priority is love. These people remind others of the Great Commandment, which emphasizes loving God first and foremost, and loving others as yourself. Again, I would agree with this statement. The Great Commandment is foundational to the entire life of the church, as God leads it. However, loving God and neighbor is not simply a feeling, or even an attitude. The book of James reminds us that genuine love moves us to action. It is never simply about words, or even emotions. Love is real when it shows itself in and through our behavior.

I believe "job one" for the church is making disciples. And you can't make disciples unless you are reaching out to those who are still without Jesus. Evangelism and discipleship are not separate objectives in the church; they are joined at the hip. In the Great Commission, Jesus Himself indicated this when He said, *"Go, therefore, and make disciples..."* (Scholars rightly indicate this is an attendant circumstantial participle attached to the verb translated "make disciples."[49] In other words, Jesus says disciple-making is (logically) connected to "going."

Moreover, disciple-making is a process word, indicating it takes time for a disciple to become a reality. The grammar of this verb suggests that process starts when the "going" reaches his or her life, not when they "pray a prayer" or "walk down an aisle." Disciple-making happens on the journey.[50]

> **Disciple-making does not stand in opposition to worship or loving God and others. Rather, it is the fleshing out of these realities in on-going life.**

Disciple-making does not stand in opposition to worship or to loving God and others. Rather, it is the fleshing out of these realities in on-going life. Since worship and glorifying God is a lifestyle, we honor and praise God with behavior that brings others to do the same. John Piper, author and pastor emeritus since 2014 of Bethlehem Baptist Church in Minneapolis, Minnesota, reminds all believers, "missions exist because worship does not."[51] And believers do not truly love God, if they are unwilling to obey His commands, including the Great Commission. These objectives are not at odds with each other, if understood holistically, rather than in a programmatic, compartmentalized way.

Does the church exist because of the mission, or the mission because of the church? Brad Brisco, author and Director of Bivocational Church Planting with the North American Mission Board of the Southern Baptist Convention, teaches ecclesiology should flow out of mission, not the other way around.[52] This is huge, and has significant ramifications on the church's life and work. If this is true, and if disciple-making is the prime objective, then how the church lives out its calling between Sunday gatherings may be more important than what happens in those hours they meet together. Some disciple-making and elements of evangelism take place in the worship experiences of churches, to be sure; however, they are slim in comparison to the impact (or lack of impact) churches make the remainder of the week outside of the hours they gather together.

Why is all of this important in this discussion on fixed expenses? Simply put, it is important because most churches spend an inordinate amount of time and money on the short experiences they have together in worship on the weekend, and very little on the majority of life lived out elsewhere. Alan Hirsch goes so far as to declare the church will discover just how much it is living out God's agenda if it will "remove the queen."[53] His allusion to the game of chess is a reminder to readers how well we are accomplishing the work and ministry of God can be seen much more clearly without the church's dependence on the weekend worship experience. For most churches that examine this, the discoveries are telling indeed.

SIMPLE IS A PLUS

By now, if you are still reading this I am going to assume I have at least given you pause. You are considering some other priority than what you have been living as a church may be a part of your congregation's necessary step forward. I have either satisfied your hesitations in implementing your church's growth through an outreach initiative, or you are at least curious to see how this reality plays out in the life of the church. Fair enough. To make forward progress then, a plan must be put in place to adjust the church's priorities and the resourcing to support them. Remember, the wisdom of Albert Einstein taught us all, "Insanity is doing things the same thing, over and over again, and expecting different results." Therefore, begin with the end in mind.

Next, how does a church make the changes necessary to adjust the budget and schedule around these new priorities and objectives? Usually, leaders are able to make some quick and easy (or, easier) changes, simply by examining the budget and the calendar for items that are not being used or supported. Other items can be eliminated that no longer support the mission of the church. Identifying and eliminating these specific elements can help in two ways: first, they will simplify the focus of the congregation and second, they will provide some needed resourcing for the growth-through-outreach efforts.

Simple is best. Simple clarifies. It focuses. It removes complexity and mitigates against confusion. Simple reduces busyness and lowers anxiety. Simple brings alignment in the church. It enables others to know what is happening and how to connect effectively. Simple produces movement.

As I argued in *PLANTED*, churches are "hoarders."[54] They have a tendency from very early in their existence to add things to their budget and calendar. They rarely, however, subtract items from one or the other. Over time these items become a part of what and how they do things in the church. These things are rarely challenged. Instead, they clutter the life of the church and cause the people to lose focus on why the church even exists. When individuals do this, we say they have a "disorder;" it is not healthy or normal.

Churches need to address this concern, too, for many of these "sacred cows" show up in the budget or on the calendar. Though they do little or nothing in helping the church accomplish its objective, these pet projects or at-one-time significant programs take up time and money to support. They sap the strength of the church and its desire for new things, since its energy is spent just maintaining these relics. They must be addressed.

> **A healthy church will spend somewhere between ten and twenty percent of its budget on outreach, ministry, and disciple-making.**

A healthy church, according to Gary McIntosh, will spend somewhere between ten and twenty percent of its budget on outreach, ministry and disciple-making.[55] In addition, ten percent more should go toward supporting missions efforts beyond the church's own efforts. Fixed expenses, including staff, benefits, facilities, utilities, maintenance, etc., make up the rest of the budget.

Calendars need to be addressed in the same way. Twenty percent of activity should be local outreach and ministry oriented, beyond the needs of the congregation itself. An additional ten percent would be ideal for missions enterprises and efforts. These items remind the church why it exists and keeps them focused on others.

After eliminating the quick and easy items from the budget and calendar that are not being used or supported by the congregation, leaders need to analyze these documents for items not supporting the priorities of the church, and especially its growth outreach initiative. Once these have been identified, learn the "back story" for each item (why they exist in the first place). Finally, start at the easiest point of leverage —where there will be the least pushback—to begin simplifying through elimination.

In many instances, you will be able to make some adjustments quickly. Aim to refocus the church through these changes. Go through the church's normal decision-making process for permission or approval, as needed. Talk to gatekeepers in advance, if it will help. Explain the rationale for the adjustments both biblically and practically, in terms of focus toward the needed objective.

Other changes will need to take place more gradually, in all likelihood. Annual budget and calendaring process can be a good time to lay preparatory steps toward other adjustments that will streamline the efforts of the church and concentrate the people on what is most important. Share the successes such changes make as widely as possible. Use testimonies and visual aids to remind and reinforce the reasons behind any new adjustments suggested. Affirm the people in the church who help these things become reality.

PROGRAMMING IS NOT A BAD WORD

In past years, church literature developed a reputation for being "pro-program." Church planting material, in particular, has argued programming is bad or distasteful[56] (even the word "program" in our denominational tribe's national funding strategy known as the "Cooperative Program" has been challenged).[57] Planters are bombarded with counsel suggesting little programming in their routine church life.

While this is widespread and understandable (I have even argued the same myself) in the life of a church plant, established churches are different in this regard, at least to some degree. Church plants are in a formative stage and because of this, need to focus more on process than program.

They are still growing and figuring out what works best for them. Planters need to resist formulaic, knee-jerk reactions, as they are often seduced in their early years to adopt simplistic, copycat methods, hoping for "quick fixes" or swift success. What is needed at this stage is the development of systems, not programs. Programs will be added later, but only if they help accomplish the objective of the system concerned.

Established churches have programming because someone at some time determined the program in question could help the church accomplish a necessary objective. Even if the program was simply copied from another church because it was cool or had tremendous results, at an intuitive level the established church implemented it because they thought it would "work." The hope was it would make a difference in the lives of people it touched. This is good.

Unfortunately, over time programs also become institutionalized. Congregants forget why programs were started and what objective they hoped to accomplish. In such instances, where they are never evaluated for effectiveness, programs develop a life of their own. The longer they are left unchallenged, the more entrenched they become. As a result, they can become more of a hindrance than a help to the church, often stifling growth that would have taken place through outreach and impact upon the community.

Because this is so, leaders of change in established churches need to find ways to have open dialogue with its members on the programming within the church. They need to ask why programs exist and have objective ways to evaluate whether they are being effective. These leaders will need patience with the people in their congregation, if they are suggesting changes to these programs; the programs in question are precious to many people within the church. And this is so with good reason: in some way these programs made a difference in their lives. The challenge once again will be helping the people desire the same result for others, even if the method needs to change.

Subsequently all of this affects the budget and calendar, as programming creates implied expectations for people in the church. As a result, it impacts how the church spends its time and money.

Resourcing should always follow strategy. Asking "what it costs" or "what time it takes" are the wrong questions. Instead asking "what is God calling us to do" is the right one. Start with the plan He has given you, then support that plan with the time and money required.

STAFFING FOR GROWTH

A note should probably be added here about staffing, too. Established churches have a greater tendency to have additional staff, beyond a lead pastor, than does a church plant. Over time, typically support staff and additional associates join a church—varying in function and number—depending on what the church feels it needs. Often these decisions are not thought through with great depth or reasoning.

For example, a typical response to the need for additional staffing in a growing church is to add a secretary and a worship pastor as soon as feasible. Normally a youth or student pastor follows. This is fairly predictable in a wide majority of American churches. However, the difficulty this presents is twofold: first, it adds to the "fixed" strain on the budget and calendar (at least if your church has teenage children), and second, it begins to tilt the focus of the church inward. These staffers serve a preponderance of their ministry internally focused on the dynamics of life within the church, not outside it.

This is no fault of their own; this is how they are gifted and blessed of God. However, the challenge it presents to the church is significant. The greater the percentage of time and money spent on the internal relationships and dynamics of church life, the less remains for those yet to be reached. Over time if not addressed adequately, the church forgets to concern itself with the needs of those in the community. They have turned inward.

This process is not easy to reverse, as new, additional staffers add to the fixed part of the budget. Time is often the only thing that will correct this, releasing more money back into the budget to be used for ministry. Often, however, this is reinvested as soon as possible in a replacement staffer who assumes the very same responsibilities, and the funds are locked up again, just as they were before.

Established churches should revisit the staffing issue every time a vacancy occurs. Determine the objective or purpose for this position. Evaluate how the last person did in accomplishing this objective. Learn the impact of this position on church life as a whole: its focus, its energy, its import. Ask whether or not a volunteer or team of volunteers can do this job, instead of a paid staffer.

This last point needs to be underscored. Established churches have a tendency to overstaff for their actual needs. Researchers say that churches need one full-time staffer for every one hundred to one hundred fifty people in a church.[58] If this is true, then eighty percent of churches need no more than two full-time staffers and likely, some administrative help. Yet, a high percentage of established churches have more than two staffers (though the additional ones may instead be part-timers, not full-timers).

> The church "learns" through experience that it can pay others to do ministry for them. This has huge ramifications for church life and the plateau or decline in years to come.

Churches like these argue that paid staffers are needed for a variety of reasons: they are more educated, polished, and capable of excellence in their field; they are dependable (could it be the paycheck?) and fulfill their responsibilities with less concern for supervision; and, they will "pay for themselves" over time through the number of people they bring into the church.

Perhaps.

However, this approach presents any church with additional difficulties, too. We have already indicated how this obligates additional funds into the "fixed" side of the budget and leaves less dollars for use in ministry. In addition, it also teaches the church a dependency upon staff that has two obvious outcomes. First, the church "learns" through experience that it can pay others to do ministry for them. By simply hiring professionally trained ministers, the church members can function to a greater degree as spectators than participants. This has huge ramifications for church life and the plateau or decline in years to come.

Second, it silently teaches the church members they don't have to (or can't) use the gifts God has given them in ministry. They don't have the expertise or education desired. So, instead of investing in the time and energy of making disciples to step into these roles, churches often find outsiders who take these positions to the detriment of the development of their own members, who slip into the background and often don't serve at all.

To be sure, there are times additional staffers are needed in a growing church. They are called of God, too. I affirm their value and the significance of what they do. I am simply advocating for the consideration of an alternative here: there may be someone(s) within your church who can serve God in these ways. In my opinion, to ignore this reality is poor stewardship, of people as well as money.

Regardless of what you end up doing, scholars suggest the best way to staff effectively for a well-rounded, healthy church is to alternate "hires" between one focused internally on the congregation and one focused externally upon the community.[59] If this is done, it keeps the church balanced in its work and ministry and avoids the danger of a staff that is servicing only the inner needs of church life within the congregation. For churches that desire to staff for growth, regardless of whether the positions are paid or volunteer, this holds the most promise for their own future.

But what happens when things fail to go according to plan? In church life, one of the most tried and true axioms is this: expect the unexpected. It is to this reality we turn our attention next.

APPLY TO YOUR SETTING

1. What does an analysis of our budget show us about our priorities? Is this in alignment with our declared vision and values?

2. What does an analysis of our calendar show us about our priorities? Is this in alignment with our declared vision and values?

3. What steps do we need to take to free up more time and money for ministry (the things that can reverse our decline)?

4. How do we staff our church? What effect has it had on our congregation?

5. How do we program in our church? What is needed, and what is not? How will be deal with the changes necessary?

QUESTIONS TO CONSIDER

1. What is "job one" for us?

2. Is our church a "hoarder" (of time and resources)? How do we address this?

3. What is our theology of staffing? The gifting of the Body of Christ?

4. How can we simplify our systems and processes?

DIGGING DEEPER

McIntosh, Gary. **Staff Your Church for Growth**. Grand Rapids, MI: Baker Books, 2000.

McIntosh, Gary and Arn, Charles. **What Every Pastor Should Know.** Grand Rapids, MI: Baker Books, 2013.

Sinek, Simon. **Start with Why.** New York: Portfolio, 2009.

Stetzer, Ed, and Im, Daniel. **Planting Missional Churches**, 2nd edition. Nashville, TN: B & H Academic, 2016.

Towns, Elmer, Stetzer, Ed and Bird, Warren. **11 Innovations in the Local Church.** Ventura, CA: Regal Books, 2007.

ENCOUNTERING THE UNEXPECTED

Pastor Stephen was caught off guard. Charles had challenged his suggestion the church use volunteer leaders with the youth group of the church, and expend the previously budgeted money for outreach into the community.

"Pastor, we need a youth director. Without it, many of our members will leave, including the Wilburns, Haleys, and Jordans. They've told me as much."

"Really?" the pastor replied. "What do they believe a staff person can do that volunteer leaders cannot?"

"Get the young people interested and involved," Charles said. "They will not show up if the leadership is simply men and women from our own church."

"I think they will," Pastor Stephen declared. "And I want us to give it a shot. This will enable us to involve the teenagers more in reaching out to their friends and schoolmates; hopefully, we will see more of them come in the days ahead, and this will help the church youth group to grow."

Charles was not convinced. He was sure the church needed a youth director; after all, First Church had always had one over the past forty-one years. If it was good enough for our parents and grandparents, it should be good enough now...

"The key to our success with the young people is not a charismatic leader or cool programming; it's caring

relationships and getting out where they are, rather than simply hoping they show up here at our building someday.

"And it is true for their parents, too; if we want to reach the families of these teenagers, it is going to depend on sharing life together with these people who are our neighbors, not in promoting some slick program. Families will have to care about families, and individuals will have to care for other individuals. This cannot happen if the community has to come here to the facility first. We must make the first effort to get the Gospel message and the love of Christ to them. We need to love them to Jesus, right where they are."

In the summer of 2006, Joyce and I had the opportunity to travel to Yellowstone National Park, the largest of the parks in our national park system. For those who are unaware of Yellowstone, it is situated at the southwestern most corner of Montana and the northwestern most corner of Wyoming. It is mammoth in size and filled with diverse wildlife. In the two short days we were there, Joyce and I saw bear, fox, antelope, deer, sheep, bison, bald eagles, grey wolf, and elk, just to name a few. It was an incredible adventure!

From the geyser of Old Faithful to one of the largest petrified forests in the world, the diversity was astounding. There was excitement around every corner! And we shared that excitement with thousands of people, who like us, sought out Yellowstone because of its almost legendary status as an otherworldly place of mystery and wonder.

One thing that caught us by surprise, though, was the unexpected and unnerving behavior of the bison. They were commonplace in certain sections of the park. For a guy like me who had never even seen them before, save in a zoo, it was exciting and scary at the same time. These bison roamed extremely close to humans; they ate grass directly beside the road. They lounged on the hillside behind us and strolled openly on the hillside. They crossed the river two hundred feet from us. One bison even came up onto the road and (thank goodness!), walked down the road away from us.

At other times we were surprised by the sudden and

unpredictable nature of humans who, traveling along, would quickly hit their brakes and crawl to a stop. They would get out of their car to look at an animal in the distance, all the while, backing up traffic down the road. Predictably, these additional tourists stopped to sightsee, as well, making it virtually impossible to move forward without patiently waiting for these humans to load back into their car and head on their way. You quickly learned to be patient and alert in navigating the roads of Yellowstone, because you could never be sure what was ahead, right around the corner.

Churches on a journey are like this, too. There are experiences unknown to leaders and members beforehand, with unanticipated adventure. There are thrills and fears along the way. There are times when it is virtually impossible to make forward progress because others are blocking the way. And there are serendipitous things to see and encounter that will keep those who experience the moment remembering it for years to come. Through it all, the one constant is to expect the unexpected, because something special, significant, and memorable could come your way at any given time.

When churches are willing to embrace a revitalization strategy similar to the one expounded in this book, there will be some unexpected surprises along the way. These surprises are both internal and external. Within the church, there will be new discoveries and allies for the journey. There will be unanticipated complications and adversaries, as well. In fact, this is true externally, as well. But the key to successful navigation of these surprises is the development of two most important elements in your strategy, ones that are arguably the most significant factors in a young church's success. And they have nothing to do with being young!

The key to your success is largely going to depend on how well your church is able to develop relationships.

GETTING TO KNOW THE NATIVES

As I wrote in my book *PLANTED*, the key to your success is largely going to depend on how well your church is able to develop relationships.⁶⁰ This seems so obvious, yet churches over time often substitute something else for the role of relationships. As a result, those who are already a part of the church come to depend upon programs, marketing strategies, and even the facilities themselves to draw people to the church. Members and attendees often become "silent partners" in the pull of the church on those-as-yet-unreached. Little is expected of the individuals actively involved already.

Church plants can't depend on programs or facilities to interest people, since they don't have these yet. They rarely have marketing efforts that attract more than an initial hearing. Instead, they have learned to depend upon the power of relationships, and they develop these to their fullest extent.

Established churches need to do the same. They must maximize the relational power of connections their members already have with others. Those who are a part of the church need to be challenged to grow the relationships toward Jesus with the people they already know. I say "toward Jesus," because it is a reality most people in our world today move closer to a relationship with Jesus one step at a time.

James Engel, in his book *What's Gone Wrong with the Harvest?*, helps us understand that individuals are on a continuum concerning Jesus.⁶¹ Engel suggested there may be as many as eight "steps" necessary to move one with no initial awareness of a Supreme Being all the way to a commitment to follow Christ. Very rarely does an individual hurdle the remaining steps (obstacles) without resolution to the previous steps in the process. If this is true, and I believe that it is for the most part, then members in our churches need to recognize their part in this life-long process within the experiences of those they know. Their objective is to join God in moving them closer to Christ, step by step. Some writers today suggest that it may take anywhere from seven to twenty-two touches to see individuals move to a place of decision.⁶²

This has huge ramifications for evangelism. Often congregants "give up" after sharing the Gospel with others two or three times. They decide others are uninterested or not under conviction from the Holy Spirit. Because they don't want to be rejected (over and over) or offensive, they simply stop sharing. Perhaps, however, members are simply failing to recognize that the people they are encountering are moving closer and closer, but only one step at a time. It is a process in which many of God's people have a part.

This starts by helping them recognize all of the relationships or connections they have with others around them. At a designated time in the life of the church, the leaders or pastor of the congregation needs to lead those present to identify individuals within their spheres of relationship. Oscar Thompson in his book *Concentric Circles of Concern* was the first I knew who encouraged Christ-followers to do this.[63] Many others have done it, as well. Thompson encouraged followers to think of a person who fits each of the following relationships in life: family member, friend, neighbor, work associate, and acquaintance (casual contact, as at the bank or grocery store, etc.), ones who are not Christ-followers and are currently unchurched. Members should be encouraged to add the names of individuals to this list also if the church member is unsure of this person's spiritual status. Identifying these individuals is critical.

After all church members and attendees have done this, leaders should encourage the people to begin praying for these relationships. This prayer needs to be daily and consistent. It should focus on their spiritual condition and the hope the member has for these individuals to come to follow Christ. If everyone in the church is doing this, then hundreds of unsaved and unchurched lives will be touched.

They should also be praying for opportunities to "grow" these relationships. We must be careful here. We are not growing these relationships simply to share the Gospel. We grow them, because people matter to God and we ought to care—even love—them. Growing these relationships will mean different things to different people, depending on their history with the person and the uniqueness of who they are individually. Some will invite a person over for tea or for dinner; others will stop by their house with a gift. Some will help them with yard work or chores; others will mail them a card. Some will invite them out to a concert or a game; others will bake them something or acknowledge a special moment of importance in their lives. The options are as varied as the people involved.

As these relationships deepen and the conversation becomes more open, opportunities will come for members to share about their God, their faith, and their church. Invitations to know more and to participate should be made. Answers to questions, while helpful, are not essential at this stage. Members can always defer to the church ("Let's ask someone at church this Sunday, how about that?"), refer them to someone else ("I'll connect you with my friend, Susan; I think she can help you with that."), or find out and get back to them with the information ("I'm not sure, but I'll find out and get back to you; how about next Wednesday?"). All of these options move the unreached and unchurched person closer to knowing Christ for themselves.

For this to work well in the life of the church, leaders need to model this for church members through their own lives. They need to share their successes and their failures. These stories will encourage and embolden others to do the same. They also remind members that they are not alone in this effort; they are a part of a larger family who is serving God together.

While this is amazingly simple and obvious, it is often overlooked in the life of an established church. Its potential is enormous. Since one of the difficulties most struggling, established churches have is identifying people they can reach, churches have a better chance of reaching and keeping individuals who already are known to have a direct connection to the church. So, build a basic outreach strategy around this.

Many non-Christians in North America don't even know a Christian, at all!

Find an ongoing way to incorporate this process of relationship-building into the life of the church. If you have a new member's class, then include the exercise and the challenge to new members there. If not, do it on a home visit, or in another way. Remember: new members are the best source of new connections with unchurched people to reach for the church. This is because almost everyone they know is currently outside the church. Don't miss this opportunity.

Sadly, I read a report in *Christianity Today* magazine recently indicating many non-Christians in North America don't even know a Christian, at all![64] Are we aware people like this are all around us? If so, what are we doing about it? The burden is on us to "go and tell," so we must see these people and build relationships with them before it is too late.

RELATIONSHIPS ARE MESSY

When established churches get serious about building relationships with others, they will discover new challenges almost immediately. The people they reach will not hold to the same values or behavior as those who have been followers of Christ in church for many years. As a result, they will think and act in ways that are unpredictable and unexpected...for believers. They will act like people without Jesus (because they often are!).

Why are churches surprised by this? Paul informs us, *"The person without the Spirit does not receive what comes from God's Spirit, because it is foolishness to him; he is not able to understand it since it is evaluated spiritually"* (1 Corinthians 2:14). In other words, the church cannot expect a person to "behave" like a follower of Christ before he or she "believes" in Christ. And neither may happen unless the church is willing to allow them to "belong" while they are deciphering the Christian Gospel for themselves. None of us can do the work of the Holy Spirit in their lives; He alone convicts them of sin, brings them to salvation, and seals them for eternity. How we act toward these people will often make them more sensitive to the Spirit's wooing or on the other hand, harden their hearts to Him.

Expect this dilemma, and deal with it in a prescriptive way. Inform the congregation what is ahead and how the church will handle the concerns. The church will need to consider how it will address the following:

- Dress code (outsiders will not necessarily dress as your members do)
- Language (outsiders will not understand church

jargon, and may even use curse words)
- Food and drink (outsiders may bring these things in places insiders would not)
- Ask questions or make comments or noise in worship (outsiders may not understand the liturgy or protocol of the church)
- Take money out of the offering plate (rare, but an outsider may do this, too!)

There are many other possibilities. The question really boils down to this: are these people whom God loves more important than our policies and norms? The answer the church gives to this will make a significant difference in your ability to reach these people with the Gospel.

DIFFICULT PEOPLE

Regardless of the answer you give to the question above, I can predict that you will encounter "difficult" people in this process. Expect them to come from both inside and outside the church, as it currently exists. Those outside the church may be easier to address than those inside, by virtue of their limited connection and relationship with the church. They could include the following:

- **The combative person** – angry and hostile toward the church (or someone in it) and/or God; they often feel betrayed; he or she has an ax to grind and may pose a physical threat to the church, becoming extremely violent in their behavior; typically, this person carries other concerns from previous or current life situations into the church.
- **The detractor** – often an atheist or agnostic, he or she is there to discourage people from coming to the church; this person is a skeptic and a cynic and attacks others mentally (not physically) with challenges to their beliefs and lifestyle.
- **The troubled person** – hurt or broken, this person usually feels the church has let them down; he or she

may have had a bad previous experience with one or more churches and this is still a barrier in their life; they may or may not have real mental or emotional difficulties; regardless, they feel alone and unloved.
- **The aggressive person** – this person is always visible, always questioning, often interrupting, and rude to others; he or she makes others feel unimportant and has poor people skills; his or her abruptness is hurtful and possibly abusive.
- **The former criminal** – this person is usually sincere and "low key" about participation in church life, at least in the early days; depending on the former crime, his or her presence will pose a considered threat to some of the people already in the church.
- **The addict** – while "polished" addicts are already in the church, appearing presentable to the congregation as a whole, it is increasingly likely that the addiction began with a legitimate medical issue; over time this person may become raw and unfiltered in his or her behavior, as well as demeanor, until their presence is unnerving to many who are already a part of the church.

It should be noted that every church, no matter if it is new or old, big or small, encounters these types of people. Their presence is not unique to a church attempting to grow through revitalization. Moreover, each of these must be dealt with individually as the church encounters them. Only the first on the list poses a serious threat to the well-being of the church. As such, security procedures need to be in place to address such needs, if problems were to occur. For the rest of these who are listed, leadership should be prepared to take appropriate action to handle each concern.

More than likely, established churches will actually encounter a greater number of "difficult" people inside the church, instead.[65] These people will tend to couch the issues they have with outsiders or with the revitalization effort in churchy language, or with religious overtones. They will likely include some of the following:

- **"They're not like us" person** – thinking more of the way the church operates, its norms and procedures, than the purpose for which it exists, this person draws a line between insiders and outsiders; often threatened by their presence and the potential it could bring, he or she will remind others that "we" are different from "them;" prejudice may be involved here, but sometimes this person is just protecting what he or she believes to be rightfully his or hers.
- **"I refuse to allow it" person** – very threatened by the presence of outsiders and the direction it will take the church in activity, expenditures, and focus, this person may attempt to hold the church hostage or hijack the vision and lead the church another way; he or she personalizes the effort and will attempt to stir up dissent and promote a lack of trust in leadership (or at least this plan from them); if influential enough (*e.g.*, a "gatekeeper"), this person could undermine the entire process.
- **"I'm against it" person** – this person simply doesn't like change and is always asking "Why should we do this?" and "What's in it for me or us?"

Of these individuals, the last is the most common and easiest to address, since most people do not like change, period. The middle one is the most dangerous to the process, and potentially to the pastor and other leaders, as he may create an insurmountable roadblock to the preferred future in their leadership. The best way to handle this person is to preempt him or her before the process starts, addressing the concerns and enlisting his or her support. But even if this person blesses the effort, leaders must communicate with him or her regularly, or suspicion will resurface, and he or she will again pose a threat.

The first person mentioned has a more serious theological and lifestyle issue that is, in most instances, rooted in sin. It is unbiblical and wrong to have an "us" and "them" mentality; Jesus broke down the dividing wall of hostility between us all (Ephesians 2:14). This issue has to be addressed over the long haul, through teaching and in person.

The point is this: relationships are messy. People are all different and while their behavior may be predictable, it can always be unexpected. The best offense is a good defense, so stay close to God, and allow His Spirit to help you as you deal with people. He will give you the words to say, if you depend on Him. But the best defense is a good offense, too! So, love people—even difficult people—with Christ's love, as best you can. *"Love covers a multitude of sins"* (1 Peter 4:8).

GET OUTSIDE THE WALLS

The second most significant factor in the church's success is getting outside of the church building and into the community nearby. This sounds easier than it is. Your church has developed a habit of depending upon its facilities to provide for the congregation almost everything it needs. You need a class? There's a room at the building. Want to plan a meal? Use the kitchen at the building. Hold a concert? There's a sanctuary at the facility. Join a sports league? Some churches provide recreational facilities on their campus. Go to school? Yes, some churches provide this, too.

Your church has developed a habit of depending upon its facilities to provide for the congregation almost everything it needs.

None of these things are bad; in point of fact, they are good. However, they present a problem: outsiders are still outside! If the church is large enough, then the facilities will be a "draw" to some in the community. But when churches are in decline, they are not the draw they used to be. Moreover, the facilities can be in disrepair and that is a turn off to outsiders, as well.

In this day and age, you cannot expect your facilities to draw the unreached and unchurched to your church, at least in the Western Hemisphere. It is going to take far more effort and initiative on the part of your members to reach them. And if they will not come to you, then the solution seems obvious: you will have to go to them. The Great Commission reminds followers of this reality, as well. So, how do we do that?

#renewbook

MEET AND GREET

The first course of community action is for the pastor of the church. He will need to set up appointments with the key community leaders who serve the residents of the church. These appointments should include, but are not limited to, the mayor, the city manager, councilmen or women, the chief of police, the fire chief, and the school superintendent. Each of these are community leaders, and they have knowledge of what is going on all over town. In addition, they are aware of specific needs that the community has and may even hope they will tackle.

For some, this may be the first opportunity to meet these key community leaders. If it is, you will want to get to know a little about them and in turn, to let them know a little about you and the church. This is not a time to draw distinctions between this key leader and your church's stance on certain issues. Rather, it is a time to build bridges of commonality and concern with the leader. It is a time to establish relationship and rapport, that will hopefully, grow over time.

The meeting does not have to last long; in fact, most leaders will be glad it is short! Take no more than 30 minutes of his or her time. Meet them at their office, and dress appropriately for the person you are seeing. Start by thanking them for the meeting and for their leadership. After getting to know a little about each other, ask them if you can gather some information from them. Make sure he or she knows that the reason you want this information is so that you and the church can help make the community a better place to live for all concerned.

Your interview should include the following questions:

- What are the most significant things (or changes) you are seeing in our community at this time?
- What excites you most about what is happening here?
- What are the biggest challenges for you?
- What are the biggest needs in our community?

- What are one of two of these needs in which you think a church like ours could specifically help you?
- How can we be a better neighbor and colleague to you in making our community better for all?
- How can we pray for you, as a community leader? (Remind them, if you need to do so, that the Bible commands you to pray for them.)

Be sure and thank the official for his or her time and the information gleaned. Give him or her your business card and let the leader know you are available for help or counsel, if you can ever be of assistance to him or her.

As a follow-up to this conversation, send the community leader a hand-written thank you note. Include your business card again, and remind him or her of your prayers. Then, evaluate the information you gleaned during the interview. Is the community seen by this leader in the same way you see it? What information needs to be shared with the church? What one or two needs can the church help the leader to tackle? How will you involve the congregation in praying for all of these leaders?

It is very important the church follow through with a plan or project to assist the community regarding at least one of the needs mentioned to them. If it does not, the community leaders will feel justified in their belief the church doesn't care or is only a critic. However, if the church will step up and help address one or two of these needs, it will aid the church's reputation among its community leaders and over time, among the community as a whole. In addition, it will dismantle the accusations and criticisms of others who see the church as judgmental and without mercy or compassion. It makes allies out of adversaries and friends out of foes.

God placed you in this location for a reason. Don't ignore it, neglect it, or try to escape it.

SERVE WITH A SMILE

Once the church leadership has this information in hand, it needs to lead the congregation to get involved in one or two projects that will get it out of the building and tackling the felt needs of the community. One or two projects are enough, especially as you begin this practice. After all, changing behavioral patterns are hard enough for a single person; for many, it can be a major challenge. So, focus on the one or two things your church can do best. Where can you make the most impact? How has God gifted you in the congregation? What opportunity has built-in motivation and appeal for your people? This is the place to start.

Rally the congregation to support this effort. Help them understand its importance in the bigger scope of things. Teach them from the Bible to care for their community. Help them realize the importance Jesus placed on mercy, justice, and compassion for those hurting and in need. Demonstrate the priority of love of God for all people through your own lives.

In addition, show them this will engender goodwill in the community and build credibility and trust. Help them see its impact on strengthening or rebuilding the church's reputation in the community. But more than anything, do this because it is simply the right, God-honoring thing to do.

God placed you in this location for a reason. Don't ignore it, neglect it, or try to escape it. God wants the church to be salt and light, and this cannot happen unless the congregation is engaging the townspeople around them. So, maximize the privileges and responsibilities this brings; commit the church to making a difference in the community. Through service in the name of Christ and through the display of love you share, lead the church to be an agent of the Spirit's transformation among the people.

I have written about this in much more detail in my last book, *PLANTED*. There I focused on the "why" of service and role these "acts of kindness" done in the name of Jesus have in the lives of God's people, as well as the community.[66] As I mentioned there, the focal point of this servant evangelism effort needs to be where the church's purpose and the community's felt needs overlap.

What kind of projects can you anticipate? There are a lot of possibilities. Communities often have the following needs, among others:

- Clean up of parks and recreational areas
- Painting of schools or other public buildings
- Repair work in dilapidated housing
- School supplies for underprivileged children
- Holiday parties for the same children

In addition, there may be community needs in senior citizen housing, community centers, daycare centers, town committees, or recreational fields. No doubt there are many other possibilities, as well. Individual needs in every neighborhood abound, from snow or leaf removal, to mowing lawns and helping fix broken fences or doors. In reality, there is no end to the possible ways a church can engage its community.

GETTING THE PEOPLE INVOLVED

I recommend you precede this process with a systematic effort to prayerwalk your community. Find a street map of your community (the town hall or planning office will likely have one), and let it guide you as you walk or drive through the community to pray for its residents. These are your neighbors! God wants you to care for them, as He cares for them.

Next, group your participants in twos or threes, and after praying for their God-given insight and safety, send them out to cover the prescribed territory for the day. Teach them to listen to the voice of God as He reveals to them the needs of their neighbors and the concerns for which to pray. These are "eyes open while you're walking by the house" prayers, so they will be brief, but hopefully impacting.

Teach the church people to pray something like this, "Father, thank you for our neighbors who live in this house. We pray as one for You to meet their needs, to make them aware of Your love and presence, and to know Jesus as Savior and Lord. If You give us the opportunity, Lord, we would be honored to serve them for You. In Jesus' name we pray, Amen." This generic prayer should be modified with the insights the Spirit brings to the group as they pass by these homes (*i.e.*, if they see toys in the yard, newspapers piled around the door, alcoholic trash in the yard, a sign suggesting a physically-disabled person lives there, etc.).

I truly believe only heaven will inform you and me of the impact these prayers make. But if I read the Bible correctly, they will indeed make an impact. God is honored by them; your dependence on Him is shown. The Enemy is put on the defensive in the lives of these people, and the Holy Spirit is asked to move in power in the town. Moreover, the people of the church will become deeply burdened for their own community, even longtime residents, some like they've never been burdened in the past.

This is why I am writing about prayerwalking in the midst of a section on gaining participation from your congregants in service to the community. The reality is churches often have trouble connecting people in service. They have programmed their members to be busy in other ways, and this new service opportunity simply sounds like additional busy work to many. Those who are mature enough already and those motivated by a strong sense of duty or obligation will join the efforts, but few others will. Prayerwalking is a simple group activity that enables the Spirit of God to motivate the Body of Christ at a heart level. It affords Him the opportunity to speak to them in a way human beings cannot. And that will make a difference.

Adding to the momentum is important. But failing to stop and celebrate, to memorialize the significance of the progress made would be a mistake.

What else is needed to involve your church members in service? Make sure the projects fit with the giftedness and makeup of the congregation. If the people in the church are white collar workers, don't suggest the church help the community with plumbing or auto mechanic needs. If the people are blue collar, tax preparation for the poor is probably not the right service effort, either. As you consider the options, connect the needs to the people of faith God has brought to the church.

Then, as lives are impacted in the community and transformation is seen, share the stories with the congregation. Let them read or hear the words of thanks and appreciation, from both community officials and those whose lives were personally touched. Members will be encouraged and motivated again to stay involved—or to get involved for the first time—as they see the difference these efforts are making. This will build excitement and give the congregation a positive sense of pride in who they are, as God's people. As a result, this will add to the momentum of outreach and growth in the church.

Adding to the momentum is important. But failing to stop and celebrate, to memorialize the significance of the progress made would be a mistake. Such moments hold great value in the lives of God's gathered people. It is this reality we address in the next chapter, as we continue our adventure.

APPLY TO YOUR SETTING

1. How are we engaging our people with their neighbors (and other concentric circles of relationships)? What steps should we take to integrate this relational strategy into our life as a church?

2. How well do we know our elected and appointed community leaders? How well do they know us? What should be our next steps in growing these relationships?

3. What community service projects can we handle that will aid the community and fuel our church in being salt and light here?

4. How are we praying for our community? What do we need to do next in this regard?

5. Are we prepared to handle difficult and troublesome people we may encounter in this process? What steps do we need to take to be better prepared for these eventualities?

QUESTIONS TO CONSIDER

1. What part does prayer play in our strategy? In our life as a church? How integral is it, really?

2. How do we show we love our neighbors?

3. What norms or behaviors are more important to us than the people God may send us?

DIGGING DEEPER

Bechtle, Mike. **People Can't Drive You Crazy If You Don't Give Them the Keys.** Ventura, CA: Revell, 2012.

Engel, James and Norton, Wilbert. **What's Gone Wrong with the Harvest?** Grand Rapids, MI: Zondervan Publishing, 1975.

Ferrazzi, Keith. **Never Eat Alone.** New York: Crown Business, 2005.

Ford, Lance and Brisco, Brad. **Next Door As It Is in Heaven.** Colorado Springs, CO: NavPress, 2016.

Pathak, Jay and Runyon, Dave. **The Art of Neighboring**. Grand Rapids, MI: Baker Books, 2012.

Shelley, Marshall. **Ministering to Problem People in Your Church.** Minneapolis, MN: Bethany House Publishers, 1985, 2013.

Sprinkle, Randy. **Follow Me.** Birmingham, AL: New Hope Publishers, 2005.

Thompson, W. Oscar. **Concentric Circles of Concern.** Nashville, TN: Broadman, 1981.

COLLECTING SOUVENIRS

The congregation at First Church had weathered the turbulence along the journey. Pastor Stephen was pleased with the way they had responded to the opportunities around them. He was also thankful they had come together as a church in dealing with the difficulties, rather than bog down in debate and indecision.

"We can almost see the light at the end of the tunnel on this journey," he reported to his Board. "It had been over two years since we started the revitalization effort, and there are several more months yet to go. The trip has been adventurous and meaningful. We have learned a lot about the community and ourselves along the way. However, we have learned more about God in this process than anyone or anything. He has been faithful, every step of the way."

"I agree, Pastor!" Board member Ed remarked. "The remarkable thing for me is seeing the community once again embrace us with open arms; our friends and neighbors are interested in our church now, and community leaders, including our mayor, call us for help and counsel. This is worth celebrating! These significant relationships are the product of genuine love and service, starting with those who mean the most to us personally. They have radiated out to the entire community, which has welcomed our efforts with heartfelt gratitude. God has given us an 'open door that no one can shut!'"

"Indeed, Ed," Pastor Stephen replied. "The journey has

reaped dividends. I'm so thankful the church didn't abandon the journey too early; they have persisted, and as a result, they have been rewarded.

"The biggest surprise to me has been the unexpected pleasures we've experienced along the way."

"What do you mean?" Caroline asked. "I don't remember any 'unexpected pleasures' that have come our way."

Pastor Stephen reminded her of the new friends and allies they now had. Some were community leaders, including the mayor, the city manager, and the school superintendent. Others were colleagues in ministry in town, both in church and parachurch organizations, who now brought synergy and purpose to joint projects within the community. Some of these were service efforts in town, but others were spiritual enterprises they jointly shared. The results were stimulating and considerable among the church memberships and the townspeople.

"At First Church, we must remember this is not about us, but about God. Because of this, I do not believe God will allow any one church to accomplish all that's needed here by themselves. We must work together in harmony, so that our ministry points people to Christ."

My wife and children know that I am a sentimentalist at heart. For friends and acquaintances beyond our family, it does not show too often. But for the Jacksons, well, that is a different story. For example, Joyce and the kids know everywhere we go on vacation, I collect a souvenir or two. Not too much, mind you, especially these days. But over the years, I have picked up these special trinkets from many different places. Something unique, something that evokes memories, and something that expresses the feelings of that one-of-a-kind place: this is important to me.

For years, the number one special souvenir for me has been a coffee mug. I have them from countless cities and states in America; I also have a dozen or so from countries overseas. In recent years, I have even had others bring me coffee mugs with the name of their country proudly displayed on the outside, because of my passion for them. At present my office is cluttered with sixty plus mugs that are never used for coffee! These mugs mean much more than a repeated hot beverage container; they are the stories of my life.

Churches that persevere in the journey toward reclaiming a vibrant, growing ministry for Christ will discover some valuable souvenirs along the way, too. They will experience moments and relationships, events and connections they will want to celebrate and cherish. These will help shape their new future.

It would be easy to assume these are nothing more than the beginning of new traditions and practices for your church. This is especially true of churches, laden with decades or centuries of rich historical efforts. But these souvenirs are not traditions, in reality; they are "markers" and mileposts along the way.

Like the "Ebenezer" of the Old Testament, these souvenirs—whether material, experiential, or relational in form—remind us of the faithfulness of God and His constant provision for His people.

Don't ever forget: God cares for your church more than anyone in it. After all, He died for it.

These souvenirs are both the mementos of this experience and the catalysts to the next stage God has in store for the church. He uses these things to remind you, convince you, challenge you, and move you forward. Seen correctly, they point His people upward to Him. They inspire a congregation to climb the next mountaintop, no matter how imposing it may seem.

So, what are these souvenirs in church life that sustain and support us? It is to this we now turn our attention.

GENEROSITY

People are more generous when growth is taking place. More precisely, people in your church will be more generous when they are led by God's vision. The power of that vision will inspire them and engage them. It will cause them to believe in His transforming power to change lives around them. It will lead them, capture them, and enthrall them. It will open their hearts to be used of God.

It has been said people give to support vision, rather than need. This is very true. Since there are needs everywhere, people want to know that their gifts make a difference. When a compelling vision engages their hearts, they are more likely to give. When their gifts show evidence of making a difference, then they will likely give more. They want their gifts to count.

Generosity starts with the heart. In a previous chapter we noted Jesus taught His disciples, *"Where your treasure is, there your heart will be also"* (Matthew 6:21). This is certainly true. Often, though, God gets the attention of people through the work He is doing around them. If and when they become aware of it, people are confronted with two options: harden their hearts or open them wider. Many among God's people will open their hearts in a greater way and give more sacrificially than before. They may also offer their time more freely than they did previously, too. This will continue to fuel the momentum forward.

One of the surprises many churches discover in times like this is non-church members will show generosity, too. This is again because they see signs that contributions are making a difference in the lives of people, or in the community at large. Churches will have to determine whether or not they will accept such gifts from non-members, and even from non-Christians, who may want to give to support a specific cause or need addressed through the church.

A related surprise is these non-members and non-Christians may volunteer their time, too, to help in humanitarian and service efforts. If your church is willing to permit their participation, they will offer their assistance, sometimes even giving up vacation time to participate in ways they know are making a difference overseas or in their own communities. These experiences can bring them into contact with the example of believers and your church; in time, they may even become believers themselves and become active in the congregation.

MAKING MORE DISCIPLES

If a church is truly reaching out into the community, it

will be impacting more lives. Over time, many of the lives touched will develop into acquaintances and hopefully, relationships. Some of them will want to know more about the church and will begin to participate in worship, fellowship, and service (as mentioned above). Through example and witness, new believers will enter into the Kingdom of God.

New believers are "trophies of His grace." As such, they are the most significant result of any revitalization effort.

These new believers are fledgling disciples; they are "trophies of His grace." As such, they are the most significant result of any revitalization effort, since their new birth impacts eternity. Your church has a "Great Commission" responsibility with these new believers; they need to be nurtured and matured in their newfound faith. They will not fully grow on their own.

New disciples can never be made solely in the classroom; while they must learn the role and importance of spiritual disciplines like prayer, the study of God's Word, witness, giftedness, and service, among other things, true discipleship requires life application. This is learned through modeling and example in their world, a kind of spiritual "on the job" training experience. So, identify and equip mature disciples in the church to work with these new believers one on one, as they come to faith in Christ.

Those you select for this ministry are very significant, for they will determine the lasting impact of this revitalization initiative. Experiences, and even relationships, come and go through life, but these new disciples last throughout eternity. As a result, this discipling ministry is likely the most important ministry your church provides. These disciplers need to live life as you desire these new believers to live life in the days and years to come. Why? Because you teach what you know, but you reproduce who you are.

Find those whose life you want reproduced in the lives of others. In the same way as the apostle Paul taught Christ-followers to *"imitate me, as I also imitate Christ"* (1 Corinthians 11:1), your disciplers will impact the "wet cement" of these new believers. They will, in turn, emulate what they see and hear in the long run, regardless of what they are taught. Theses disciplers serve as mentors to them, helping these young believers to grow strong in their walk with Christ.

This requires you to plan for two eventual consequences: first, the priority of this role in the lives of your key disciplers above other responsibilities they have in church life; and second, the understanding that a "disciple" is not made when he or she masters a body of knowledge, but when they in turn reproduce other disciples. For these consequences to take place, leadership must adjust roles and expectations for these members. Sadly, most churches don't do this; instead, they just expect these members to add the discipling role to other responsibilities they already have.

Because mature disciples are serving in some capacity already, something will suffer. For some, their previous, on-going ministry will be slack. For others, they will neglect the discipling responsibility they've been given. And for yet others, they will "burn out," trying to do everything instead of prioritizing the most important thing. None of these results are good or acceptable, so plan ahead of time for this. How will you conserve the fruit of your outreach efforts? This needs to be a key decision in your preparation.

This is a key reason some plateaued and declining churches refuse to plan for growth again. They know making disciples is time-intensive and cannot be rushed. They know they do not have enough leaders now to do all they have in mind, much less add this responsibility to church life. So, they choose not to grow, as it will compromise their current way of doing things. It will require change that they do not want to make, since the system will not be able to remain the same. This is sad and unfortunate.

Stephen Covey taught us to "begin with the end in mind."[67] If disciple-making is the mandate from our Lord, then it has to be the prime directive for His church. How can the church not prepare for this eventuality? God will not bless our efforts when our agenda differs from His own. Churches must adjust their priorities to place disciple-making at the top.

In addition, disciplers and those whom they disciple need to understand the process is not complete until the new disciple has in turn discipled another person, passing along the knowledge and the process to others who can repeat it themselves (2 Timothy 2:2). At the last church I planted, our slogan, *"Making Disciples and Sending Them Out,"* reflected this value. The process will end, if it is not reproducible and transferred to others.

LEADERSHIP DEVELOPMENT

Reaching new believers and discipling them will require additional leaders for the church. Seriously, is there any church that does not need more leaders? In many ways, they are the life blood of the church's progress. If the church has enough leaders, it is growing; if not, the church is stalled or declining. For a church to engage the community successfully, leaders will be needed. The good news is this: growth through outreach to the community will often uncover more potential leaders, as well.

Leadership pulls from the fringes. It needs to find potential among those who have not yet been grafted into the integral systems of the church.

This happens in two specific ways. As the current leaders of the church are refocused on new priorities, including disciple-making and outreach to the community, others already inside the church will have opportunity to step into their previous ministry roles. Negatively, this "glass ceiling" in church life is all too real for those who are not longtime members of the church. It often stalls the development of younger members. More importantly, it cools their passion for service, so that many end up becoming only spectators in church life.

Leadership pulls from the fringes. It needs to find potential among those who have not yet been grafted into the integral systems of the church. Discipling these individuals now enables them to use their giftedness in ministry for the Body.

Secondly, as new people in the community are reached, come to be followers of Christ, and grow as disciples, they can be moved into the leadership pipeline. Using the "Paul-Timothy" method, they first watch a mature leader model leadership skills. Next, they assist the leader in implementing that skill. Then, the leader assists them as they implement the same skill. Finally, the leader mentors this "Timothy" as they handle it on their own. If successful, the new leader will be released and empowered to work the process with someone else.

John Maxwell said in a conference I attended many years ago, the key to having enough leaders is never doing anything alone.[68] Create a process in your church's life that reflects this reality and you will continually be developing these new leaders. This expands the ministry of the church and it matures growing disciples.

FOR THE SAKE OF THE KINGDOM

Churches involved in positive revitalization are pleasantly surprised to discover a significant change in the relationships they have with other churches in the community. The churches that preach the Gospel message will celebrate the impact they are making, while those who are not evangelical often create some resistance to their efforts. Both results merit a discussion.

Evangelical churches in the community will become allies in the process of reaching more people for Jesus. Effective church plants discover this early in their genesis; likeminded churches are not "the competition." As a result, they will collaborate on community projects that will benefit each one of their congregations. They will support each other in prayer. They will find additional ways to partner together or assist each other in ministry, as needed. Cooperative work will be shared as denominational or local church polity allows.

Non-evangelical churches tend to feel differently, however. They tend to resist the desire for cooperative efforts (a lone exception may be a Good Friday service, which seems to be common in many places). Frankly, they often consider new churches unnecessary and evangelism out-of-date. Though I recognize I am speaking in sweeping generalizations, these churches tend to be older and more tradition-laden, with a rich community history. However, this same history often encumbers them in the present, as least in regards to growth.

They tend to be declining or at least plateaued.

New churches have found that the churches engaged in cooperative efforts with other congregations in the community, whether they be with churches within their own tribe or with other denominations, tend to grow effectively. At first glance, this seems counter-intuitive: how could helping others or sharing resources facilitate growth? The answer is twofold. Joining other congregations in Kingdom ventures honors God and reminds everyone the Church belongs to Him. He sets the agenda and determines whom He will use. It also reminds the local church why they are here and the reality that God is not going to share His glory with anyone. No one church will accomplish everything needful; thus, only God can get the glory.

Second, these efforts overcome selfishness, which often begin to guide a church's own decisions and resources as the church ages. Instead, by unselfishly looking beyond themselves and trusting God who is the Source of their ministry, such efforts focus them on Jesus, the Head of the Church, and teach them through experience to count on His provision. This in turn provides a powerful witness to the community at large of the Body of Christ, acting in unison for Kingdom purposes.

LEGACY PLANTING

Another counter-intuitive ministry possibility, which brings blessing and vitality to a plateaued or declining church, is planting or parenting a new church. This opportunity is usually met with fear by struggling churches (though even growing churches sometimes are concerned about its impact on their efforts, too). However, it can be one of the greatest blessings a church experiences even during a revitalization effort.

Why? There are many reasons this is true. It causes the church to live again by faith and not settle simply for comfort or the status quo. In so doing, God teaches them new lessons of dependence and His provision. It also brings excitement to the church as their collective pulse beats a little faster over the difference the church is making through sacrificing for the benefit of the new "baby" church. They see the impact and hear the stories; these add value to their own congregation's life and ministries.

The rewards are great. Think of it as an investment, both in others and in the future. Lives are changed and another community begins to be transformed. Or it may be that your church chooses to go to another part of your own community and begin a multisite venture, which reaches new people with the Gospel who would never come to your church building. Or perhaps your congregation sees the need to reach another people group in the area, who do not primarily speak your language. Through your effort in church planting, the Kingdom will invade new cultures and new ethnicities to bring Gospel transformation.

> **Think of it this way: why would God want to send anyone--created in His image whom His Son died to redeem-- to your church, if you refused to reach others you could with the Gospel?**

Think of it also as part of the legacy your church establishes for years to come. In this way the church grows broader, not just larger, as it extends the Kingdom beyond a single place and time in which you are currently living. Is this not worth the effort, in order to leave a greater impact on the world for Jesus, to make a more significant difference others can experience for decades or centuries to come?[69]

Assisting a new church also brings God's blessing with your obedience. Think of it this way: why would God want to send anyone created in His image, whom His Son died to redeem, to your church, if you refused to reach others you could with the Gospel? As a father, I would not want that for anyone for whom I care, much less my own children. In the same way, God is looking for those who will honor Him by living responsible, obedient lives of service for Him.

MOMENTS IN TIME

Other souvenirs the congregation collects during this process include the "God moments" that occur, because of the revitalization initiative. A significant life may be transformed through the church's efforts (*e.g.*, the mayor, the police chief, etc.). The community may even recognize the church for its efforts and honor it is a special ceremony or with a special memento. An historic event (anniversary, commissioning, etc.) may take place during this time period that further fuels the congregation forward and marks the effort with a critical milepost to be remembered and celebrated for years to come. The possibilities of these "Ebenezer" experiences are endless.

However, they can be missed or ignored if your leaders are not watching for them. So, be alert! God is confirming His presence and securing His provision for the church in a variety of ways to affirm the church's efforts. He invites the church to join Him in further opportunities as they follow Him on the journey.

EXCEEDINGLY ABUNDANTLY BEYOND...

I have added this final subsection to remind everyone God constantly does far more than we could ever ask or imagine. It is His nature; it is His heart's desire (Ephesians 3:20). As a result of this reality, churches can never make a final determination on how—or how much—God will bless their efforts. If they attempt to determine all God is going to do or how He is going to act based on only what they see, they will always underestimate Him. If the church attempts to analyze the productivity of an effort solely on the basis of profit or loss, the analysis will fall woefully short of divine reality. The results and the impact can never be fully known this side of eternity. Because this is true, what our minds and senses tell us will never be the whole story. We cannot make our decisions on this basis.

Throughout history, God has a habit of taking our "little" and making it result in His "much." He did it with Gideon's army, with David's sling, with the lad's five loaves and two fishes. He wants to do it with us. When we are willing to honor God with an effort at growing His kingdom, just wait and see what God wants to do in your midst. It will be something your church will be sharing with your children, and with your children's children. It will be exceedingly, abundantly beyond anything you could ask or imagine.

APPLY TO YOUR SETTING

1. The author lists at least five "souvenirs" a church can experience in the process of revitalization: generosity, more disciples, leadership development, Kingdom partnership, and church planting. Which of these has resulted in your revitalization effort? How has that been celebrated? What next steps are needed to deal with these significant results?

2. What "God moments" have been evident as a part of this journey? What have they taught you about God? What about His work in our lives?

3. What other "exceedingly abundantly beyond" results have you seen or experienced? As you reflect on these results, what conclusions have you drawn?

4. What are previous "Ebenezers" in the life of your church? Does the church know what they mean? What God did? Why or why not?

QUESTIONS TO CONSIDER

1. Are we willing to trust God beyond what we can see? Why or why not?

2. How are we pausing to commemorate the milepost moments of God's work in our midst?

3. How can God use us to change the world? Are we willing to do "whatever it takes?"

DIGGING DEEPER

Harrington, Bobby and Patrick, Josh. **The Disciple Maker's Handbook.** Grand Rapids, MI: Zondervan Publishing, 2017.

Katz, Judith H. and Miller, Frederick A. **Opening Doors to Teamwork & Collaboration.** San Francisco: Barrett-Koehler Publishers, Inc., 2013.

Malphurs, Aubrey. **Building Leaders.** Grand Rapids, MI: Baker Books, 2004.

Moore, Ralph. **Starting a New Church.** Grand Rapids, MI: Baker Books, 2002.

Sparks, Paul, Soerens, Tim and Friesen, Dwight J. **The New Parish.** Downer's Grove, IL: InterVarsity Press, 2014.

Tozer, A. W. **The Attributes of God, Volumes 1 & 2.** Chicago: Wing Spread Publishers, 1997, 2001.

#renewbook

ARRIVING AT YOUR DESTINATION

 The people of First Church had gathered for a service of celebration. Through the efforts of the past thirty-six months, God had done incredible things, both in and through them. Dozens of new believers had been reached with the Gospel and were now being discipled by the church. Vantage Point, a new church plant, had been started by the combined efforts of First Church and Redemption Fellowship, where Pastor Joe, now a good friend of Pastor Stephen, ministers. The Mayor and the school superintendent were constantly communicating with Pastor Stephen about new ways First Church could help the residents of the community with needs that had to be addressed. Transformation was happening!
 This was true inside the church, too. New believers meant First Church was seeing a reversal of the downward decline of the past twenty years. Additional leaders were surfacing, and new ministries were forming around the fresh, unifying vision God was revealing to Pastor Stephen and the church. The people were more sacrificial, more generous, more willing to step out in faith, and by all appearances, more blessed. God had made this happen; they had simply— but profoundly—chosen the hard work of obedience. Though not easy or comfortable, it had made all the difference. First Church was making an impact in their world again.
 "Ladies and gentlemen, this is a monumental day in the life of our church," Pastor Stephen announced. "Today we stand here united before God, giving thanks to the Almighty for what He has made possible. He gets all the glory, for without Him, all that we have done would be utterly empty

and void of meaning.

"*And to you who are a part of First Church, I want to tell you how proud I am to be your pastor. You have served faithfully and wholeheartedly. Even in the tough, difficult moments on this journey, you followed God's lead. Moreover, you were willing to think outside of the box, trying creative and innovative things new to us, so that others could be reached with the Gospel. And it has made a difference.*

"*The inhabitants of heaven will be greater because of your love and service; the inhabitants of hell fewer, because you cared.*

"*And now we stand at the destination point, where we sought to land when we started this journey. Together we mark the significance of this sacred moment. Here we raise our 'Ebenezer,' for 'hitherto, the LORD hath provided for us.' Let us never, never, never forget this valuable lesson! For God did not join us on this journey; rather, He invited us to join Him...and we did!*

"*Can anyone here tell me why we should end such a rich and meaningful journey? Instead, may God show us a new destination that will propel us forward in an even greater way than before, and may we respond in eager obedience, like never before.*"

Seven years ago my wife, Joyce, and I were in the final throes of one of our European vacations. We had left Florence, Italy, and changed Eurorail trains in Milan. We were headed for our final destination in Zurich, Switzerland. We looked forward to the big city and the quaint villages nearby. Joyce had never visited Switzerland previously, and I wanted to show her the awe-inspiring beauty in this small, but special country.

This leg of our train ride began in spectacular fashion, as we headed in a circuitous route through the Alps bordering Italy and Switzerland. Even in September, there was large evidence of snow on these higher elevations. I was taking photographs right and left, recording the scenic views for posterity.

The gorgeous landscape soon gave way, though, to an

unexpected obstacle: the railroad tracks were "out" a mile or so further toward our destination. This meant a detour was in order, and so the train squealed to a stop at the station in Biasca, Switzerland. We all disembarked from the train in this Italian-speaking village and were herded onto buses to transport us past the barrier. The delay was long and frustrating for us, as we know only a few words in Italian. The journey, which had started in such a spectacular way, had turned difficult.

Soon, the buses had reunited us with the train, safely beyond the obstacle to our adventure, and once again we were speeding toward Zurich, our terminal destination. As we entered the train station in this greatly significant European city, all thoughts of the complications earlier in the day were gone. We had made it! Now, we were on our way to discovering central Switzerland, what some people call the most beautiful region in the world.

Getting "there" is the ultimate desire of most travelers when they journey. Certainly, I have suggested already in this book that the destination is where you desire to head with all focus and deliberation.

But I've also suggested you must not solely value the destination, but rather, enjoy and embrace the journey, as well. There will be lessons learned and moments experienced that will impact for a lifetime, if you refuse to hurry past these mileposts, and if you pause long enough to soak in the view. Still, the destination is your goal and to that we now turn our attention.

ADAPTIBILITY AND CREATIVITY

Obstacles and roadblocks are the stuff of life. All of us encounter them from time to time. No matter how well you have planned and prepared for the future, someone or something will throw you a curveball in an attempt to strike you out. Two ingredients are necessary for you to navigate successfully the treacherous waters of change: adaptability and creativity.

Adaptability, and its close brother flexibility, is natural for church planters. Planters have the God-given makeup to change directions quickly, as circumstances demand. Their lives in this regard are somewhat unique; since they create things from nothing, or worse, out of chaos, they have an inborn ability to improvise on the fly. This is not necessarily true of pastors who are leading an established church on a revitalization journey.

Typically, these leaders detail a plan, gain its appropriate approval for implementation, and then work the plan. When unanticipated situations arise, those with stringent detail and complex processes are slowed down. In addition, their church structural systems may require that permission be granted from the Board or the congregation before additional adaptations can be made. These elements are part of the reason adaptability is difficult for the church. Moreover, many pastors adjust slowly, too, and this further complicates the matter. The only certainty in the plan is that it will need to adapt.

> **This is a given reality for all revitalization projects; since the environment in which the church ministers is changing, the plan will have to change, sooner or later, too.**

This is a given reality for all revitalization projects; since the environment in which the church ministers is changing, the plan will have to change, sooner or later, too. The better the leaders handle the necessary adjustments, the easier it will be to reach the destination. So, if the pastor of the church is not a capable adapter, or it is not the church's "cup of tea," then find others who can be trusted within the leadership circle who are good at this. Inquire of them about ways to revise the plan for greater success and impact.

In addition, church planters tap into a great deal of creativity and innovation in effective new church starts. They think "outside the box," if they use a box, at all! This leads to innovation, catalyzing significant impact in ministry. Why? Most people are creatures of habit, and quickly settle into a routine with which they are comfortable. Just think about how quickly and consistently the people of the church sit in the same places during worship each time they attend! Routine has its value, but not with unchurched people. Typically, the routine in place—the pattern of worship, the way outreach happens, the means of ministry, etc.—is not attractive or beneficial to them. On a rational basis, this is part of the reason they stay away.

New wineskins are needed for new wine. Effective church planters create new ways of doing things that break down the barriers of routine and get past the obstacles of the obvious. They transcend the expected and find novel, fresh ways to touch lives with the Gospel. This is compelling and is not met with resistance or defensiveness by the unchurched, because it has been unanticipated. Often, it is even enjoyed and connects with them, since they do not know how to think in the conventional ways of most churched people. It speaks to them.

For an established church to arrive at its destination, creativity will be needed. Ask questions like, "How else could we do this?" and "What would get the attention of those we are trying to reach?" The answers to these questions create innovative means of building bridges to those who need Jesus.

If innovation is not strong among the church's leaders, find others who are. They are often found at the fringe or peripheral of traditional church experience. They may be younger people or new members to the congregation. Glean insights from them by asking questions on how to connect with outsiders, or even their own friends who are not yet involved with a church. If the church still struggles to find ways to engage the unchurched within the community, then read what others are doing. There are many sources that can share options and alternatives for consideration.

However, the implementation of innovative strategies in the community must be true to the identity of the church, motivating the congregation and resonating with the unchurched in the community. All three of these things are keys to success. First, be genuine. If the idea or creative way presented to the community seems fake, artificial, or simply not "you," then do not do it. Find a way that exemplifies the personality and style of the church more accurately. Second, the church should get excited about the means of serving and conveying God's grace that has been selected. If it does not impassion them, it will not excite those they are trying to reach. Finally, choose a method that will gain attention and also connect with the community. Use an approach the townspeople will appreciate and embrace, based on who they are (their own unique personality).

Obviously, this is not an easy task; it requires much prayer, thought, and dialogue. However, by being adaptable and creative, the pastor and leadership can overcome most of the barriers the church may confront on this journey.

CELEBRATION

Arriving at the destination will bring joy and relief. The congregation will rejoice that it has achieved something significant for God. In some cases, this will be the first time the congregation has had this kind of impact in many years. Regardless, they will be enthused and excited at the accomplishment; more importantly, they will rejoice because God has used them in the process.

This reality goes deep into the psyche. It affirms identity (who we are in God's kingdom work) and purpose (why we are here). It should not be ignored, but parlayed into a better, richer, deeper understanding of what God is doing in His Church (with a capital "C") and the local congregation's role in it. These results will enhance self-esteem and value for them; it will promote the faithfulness of God and the willingness of the church to trust Him. It will mold their collective, impressionable mind, with new realities of God's provision and their usefulness. It will enlarge their heart for Him and for others.

If the church does not pause…it may be perceived as viewing its hard-working membership as objects rather than persons.

These are all reasons to celebrate. This is a necessity, not an option! Find a way to commemorate the completion of the plan and the fulfillment of the project. A worship experience, followed by a fellowship party, is best. Make it a poignant moment in the life of God's people, as they celebrate Him and the privilege He has given the church to join Him on this adventure. Acknowledge the transforming encounters the church and community have experienced along the way. Commemorate new relationships with Christ-followers and community leaders that have become significant as a part of this journey. Tell stories and show digital photos or videos. Cheer and applaud God, and those who are the fruit of this effort.

Too many churches in the world today miss the significance and importance of celebrating God's work among them. They rush on to the next thing, quickly forgetting what God has done and the difference it has made. Do not let that happen here! A celebration experience "marks" the church; it creates a moment of closure in joy, but also a motivation for doing it again.

This joyful response is joined by a response of relief. For many who have not seen a growth initiative like this in years, the experience though meaningful, has taxed them. They have felt like they were climbing uphill the entire time. The process has produced goals, preparation, events, and efforts that have kept them focused and deliberate—even busy—over the past many months. For these people, the destination point causes them to give a collective sigh. They are satisfied and pleased with the results, but it has been hard work. Now they desire to rest.

This is not a bad, nor a totally inappropriate, response. Certainly, if the church does not pause, it will not take the needed opportunity to acknowledge what has happened here. In addition, it may be perceived as viewing its hard-working membership as objects, rather than persons. Remember, the Bible says rest is needed,[70] so relief can be good. As long as the congregation does not settle into complacency, it can bring restoration to the souls of those needing it. This adds to greater productivity (much like a vacation is intended to do for you personally) down the road.

RECALIBRATION

The journey has ended. Obstacles have been overcome. The destination has been celebrated. What is next for the church, at this point? Good question.

Several things come to mind. The church needs to be refreshed. Rejoicing is integral to this moment in church life, but relief is a part of this, too. Relaxing the strain of ministry is not ineffective or inconsequential. It is like going down the other side of the mountain. It is eventually necessary for further progress to be made.

This restoration process puts the focus on recalibration. The church does this through evaluation and then, re-dreaming the dream. It is as though someone has reached the top of the mountain and can look back to see from where he or she has come. In addition, the individual can look forward to see where one can head next. Perspective permits this from the current vantage point.

The evaluation process begins with a review of the strategic plan used by the church for the process. What happened? Who participated? Where did the church have to make necessary changes? Why? These questions and others help the church to be wise stewards of time and money in the future. It also conserves the results of the experience, which will benefit others who follow them.

Evaluation also includes surfacing and recording the lessons learned from God during the process. It records this truth for posterity, but also to reinforce and remind the current congregation of how God is at work in their midst. It promotes further opportunities to grow in relationship with Him through discipleship and service.

Evaluation notes the bad as well as the good, in an attempt to keep from repeating mistakes previously made. It should be honest, fair, but relentless in obtaining the truth from as many perspectives as possible. With this in mind, hearing from leaders, lay people, staff, new members, and even outsiders will assist the church as it makes further decisions about the future.

Re-dreaming the dream is bathed in prayer; it is first a call to greater dependence upon Him, then action for Him.

In addition to evaluation, the pastor and leaders should look forward from this new vista point. Now that the church has reached this place, what is God revealing? Where does He want the church to head? What is needed for the next adventure? Who will go? When will the church be ready?[71]

Re-dreaming the dream is bathed in prayer. It involves waiting on God for His direction. It is first a call to greater dependence upon Him, then action for Him. The time in prayer is a time of refreshment for the soul. It reenergizes the tired and weak; it refocuses the head-strong and too eager. It reminds all involved that the people move at His agenda, not their own.

A new vision will issue forth out of a relationship saturated in prayer and dependency on God. He will show His people what comes next. While I don't know what that will be, I can assure you of certain things:

- It will build on what the church has already done for God
- It will use the giftedness and uniqueness of the church
- It will involve disciple-making and other unreached people, beyond those now touched by the congregation
- It will honor God and bring Him glory, not the church itself
- It will involve something that cannot be accounted for in human terms; in other words, God will have to show up for it to be accomplished

This new vision should be introduced with passion, motivation, and excitement to the congregation, as was done previously. It should be conveyed as God's new opportunity for the congregation to join Him in something else of eternal significance. The church should see it as a privilege and sign of His blessing, not an obligation or hardship.

How much time should pass between the last focused initiative and this new one? It is impossible to say with any accuracy, for timing is more an art than a science. There are too many variables at work, including the leadership style and strength of the pastor, the season of the calendar year, and how long it took to complete the last journey. Those within the process will "feel" this at a heart level. Certainly, some time is needed for the above items mentioned. But even then, through evaluation, prayer, and planning, the church is already at work recalibrating for the soon-to-be-realized next journey of eternal significance.

    This is important. God has His church here for this very reason, and our work will not be finished on earth before the Bride of Christ is united with Him in heaven. Until that time, we journey onward and upward for Him! For "our hope is built on nothing less than Jesus' blood and righteousness."[72]

APPLY TO YOUR SETTING

1. What adaptations need to be made to our understanding of the plan God has given us on our journey? What innovations? Who needs to help us determine this?

2. How do we plan to celebrate our arrival at the determined goal? Who needs to be involved in this?

3. What evaluation is needed of the lessons learned? The successes experienced? The mistakes made? The resources and manpower expended?

4. How do we rest and recalibrate for the future? How do we "bless" this effort without allowing complacency to settle over the congregation?

5. What is God revealing to us about our future from here? What will we do with this knowledge?

QUESTIONS TO CONSIDER

1. Do our processes and procedures value adaptation and innovation? If not, what needs to change?

2. How important is evaluation to us? How do we do this?

3. When do we celebrate? What is its value to us as a church?

DIGGING DEEPER

Biehl, Bob. **MasterPlanning.** Nashville, TN: B & H Publishing, 1997.

Klopp, Henry. **The Ministry Playbook.** Grand Rapids, MI: Baker Books, 2002.

Malphurs, Aubrey. **Advanced Strategic Planning,** 3rd edition. Grand Rapids, MI: Baker Books, 2013.

McFayden, Kenneth J. **Strategic Leadership for a Change.** Lanham, MD: Rowman & Littlefield, 2009.

CANCELING THE TRIP
(An Alternative Ending)

Pastor Stephen hung up the phone. He was dismayed. The leader of his Board had just given him the bad news. The church leadership had decided NOT to proceed with the efforts to reach out to the community or bring growth within First Church. They had determined that the cost was too high, not just in dollars, but in time, energy, and manpower. The leadership felt it could not afford to sacrifice these items without hurting the life of the current church members. This was a higher priority to them than those out in the community who were lost and unchurched.

The pastor had attempted to refocus their eyes outward, but had struggled. "Things will turn around, Pastor," Ken, one of the key leaders in the church told him. "There is no need for us to change what we're doing. We just need to work at it harder and better. After all, you know First Church: we like the way we do things around here and are not too positive about change."

Stephen noted the lack of urgency in Ken's words. He was convinced the situation was more serious than Ken realized. If action was not taken soon to reverse this trend, the church would continue to dwindle in number and in impact. In addition, the situation would become even more grave, and thus, more difficult to turn around.

"I believe it was Albert Einstein who said, 'Insanity is doing the same thing over and over again, and expecting

different results,'" Pastor Stephen said. "Some things must change or the church will become increasingly irrelevant to the rest of the world, and maybe even, cease to exist."

"Oh, Pastor," Ken replied, "you're overreacting; it's not that bad. We're First Church. We're not going anywhere. As long as we're here, people will come. We'll be fine. And as for the community, they know where we are located; if they want us or need us, they'll let us know."

The pastor's heart sank. He thought to himself, how did the church get so far from heart of God? Where is the concern for the lost and for our community? I have given my life here for the past nine years, and this is the result?

Suddenly, the alarm clock went off. Pastor Stephen was awakened by the startling, intrusive sound. He abruptly sat up in bed. He looked around in the dark, for any signs of normalcy. It had only been a dream...a nightmare, really. Thank goodness, he thought, that scary dream isn't reality for us. I hope it's not reality for anyone, he thought.

In February of 2010, I was preparing to attend the first-ever Verge Conference in Austin, Texas. This much-anticipated event, featuring Alan Hirsch and Francis Chan, promised new learning and powerful networking possibilities for me in my ministry. And an additional caveat for me was I would be able to visit Austin, Texas, where everything is weird, by their own admission. (Austin is one of those places in America on my own "bucket list.") I had made all the arrangements for the trip—conference registration, the plane ticket, the hotel and car reservations—and had packed my suitcase for a quick departure for the airport the following morning. What I had not counted on, though, was a lack of cooperation from the weather.

I awakened on February 4 in the suburbs of Baltimore to the middle of a snowstorm the *Washington Post* came to call "Snowmeggedon."[73] Overnight our area had been blanketed by over a foot of snow; the storm didn't stop until it reached thirty plus inches. Currently, though, it was only twelve to fifteen inches deep...hey, I could still make my flight, right?

Wrong. The Baltimore-Washington International Airport had come to a screeching halt, a virtual ghost town. It had closed to all traffic. Moreover, I couldn't get out of my own driveway, regardless. The streets had not been cleared, and since we lived on a very low-priority street, there was little chance I would be able to do so, for perhaps a day or two.

I was snowed in. My trip was canceled. I wasn't going anywhere.

My disappointment was only part of the consequences. Though I was able to watch the sessions from home and learn some helpful things, thanks to live streaming video, I was unable to network with those present on behalf of my ministry organization. I was unable to recoup all of the expenses invested in the arrangements for the trip. And I missed out on seeing Austin, a place that continues to remain on my bucket list to this day.

Canceling trips are fraught with complications. They leave a wake of "loose ends" that must be handled. They produce unwanted emotions and attitudes that bring collateral damage. They affect others beside yourself. And, of course, they do not get you to your destination.

When a church commits to a strategy, planning to reach out into the community and make a difference, it will test their resolve. There will be complications and unexpected situations that arise. There will be obstacles and detours that must be taken. There will be criticism and challenges along the way. And there will be the temptation to quit.

There are many reasons a congregation or its leadership may choose not to start a revitalization journey. I have tried to address some of these concerns in the earlier chapters of this book. However, there are some that may surface after you are in the process itself. And though the membership agreed to move forward, the unimagined results may leave them reconsidering their previous decision. I've listed some of the possible motives for canceling the journey below.

"WE DIDN'T REALLY WANT THIS"

This declaration deals with the consequences of change on the life of the congregation, particularly the ones making such a statement. They are not enjoying the changes taking place, in part, because it is change and in part, because of the consequences. We have addressed the issue of change in the third chapter of this book. Let me say it again: most people do not like change. Since it is a constant in life, they accept change, often begrudgingly when it is forced upon them. However, their clear preference is to avoid it altogether. People tend to like things the way they are, since it provides them some stability in the midst of an ever-changing world.

> **Change will bring results. These results will include unintended consequences.**

This stability, though, manifests itself in the form of comfort at some point. Because of this, change is seen as the enemy, since it attacks not only our need for security in life, but rather, our ability to enjoy that life, on our own terms, the way we like it. Such comfort finds allies in those who have accepted these norms as their own and are also along on the journey. They are rejected, though, by others who are on the outside, or who resist the values or norms they express.

Comfort, for comfort's sake, must be challenged by leadership at some point. People must be reminded comfort is a want, not a need. Churches must be concerned about meeting needs first before wants.

In addition, change will bring results. These results will include some unintended consequences: parking lot problems, guests sitting in the preferred sanctuary seats of longtime members, scheduling adjustments, etc. Members may wonder what is happening, and if they are getting more than they wanted.

If your church is successful at reaching new people, and they, in turn, become a part of your church, then at some point the "natives will become restless." Carl George and Bob Logan in their book *Leading & Managing Your Church* talk about the fact every church has two distinct strata of people within the congregation. There are the natives, who these authors call "formerberries," ones who have been there a long time, including charter members. These people are in many ways the pioneers who have borne a lot of the burden of making the church what it is today. They have sacrificed and served to shape it into its current fashion. They have established the culture of the church, and are typically, leaders and gatekeepers in the congregation.

Then, there are the "newberries" ("immigrants" into the congregation), those who are new to the church and have transplanted into the congregation more recently. These individuals bring with them their own ideas and dreams of how the church should deal with virtually everything. They see things differently, often in a more functional way, because they are concerned with why it is done, not just how it is done.[74]

If your church is successful at reaching new people through this revitalization effort, sooner or later you will have enough new voices to challenge the status quo. This kind of change causes many churches to back away from growth as a desired outcome. It causes them to settle for the way things are.

Leadership, especially the pastor, have to respond to this in several ways. First, there is the biblical mandate. Every believer must be accountable for the authority of God's Word on his or her own life, as well as the life of His church. Pastors need to point the people to the need for obedience to Scripture, as it guides God's people on their journey. Second, there is the sociological reality. Groups are challenged in intimacy, role, and importance by outsiders as their number enlarges the Body of Christ. Old-timers will feel challenged in their relationships (intimacy), their positions (role), and their authority or power (importance) by newcomers who make their presence known and assimilate into the congregation. Leadership has to educate the longtime members about these realities before they happen, and they have to welcome newcomers who want to incorporate into the life of the church.

"THIS IS TOO COSTLY"

As the journey continues, there may be people within the congregation arguing the effort is costing too much. This statement is evidence of a current dissatisfaction by those saying it. They may truly be unhappy with the expense of the process; however, they may be expressing something more, instead. Members who say this may be indicating the price is more than they are willing to bear.

What price, you ask? Their giving is a part of this concern, to be sure. They worry about the impact new initiatives have on the current budget and priorities. Typically, struggling churches do not have a lot of excess money. When new initiatives are implemented, then other things may suffer. These may be items of personal interest to those who hold this concern.

However, these members may be just as concerned about the price they are paying now for what is yet to come. They don't want to mortgage the present for the future.

Since more people live in the present or the past than the future, and since a majority of members in declining churches are older in age anyway, these people feel this to be a legitimate, personal need. The cost in tradition, memories, and the like, hits home for them, too.

The pastor and leaders in the church need to remind members of the price Jesus paid for us all, even those as yet still unreached. The cost of quitting the process is actually much higher. Stopping the process means lives go unreached, the community goes unchanged for Jesus, and likely, the church remains in continual decline. Which results are really costlier?

"IT'S TOO HARD"

Revitalization takes hard work. It may be a labor of love, but it is labor, nonetheless. Members must participate for it to be successful, and even then, it will be yeoman's work. It requires focus and energy; it will be strenuous and tiring. And it will take time. It is not a quick fix or instant answer.

Leadership will bear the brunt of the heavy lifting...but the rest of the membership will have to join in the process, for it to be successful.

Leadership will bear the brunt of the heavy lifting. They must expect many hours, agonizing in prayer and hard work, both preparing and implementing the plan. But the rest of the membership will have to join in the process, for it to be successful. The initiative depends on full involvement and participation of the church. By full, I am suggesting sixty to eighty percent of the active ongoing church family, almost a reversal of *Pareto's Principle*.75

This helps lighten the load for everyone, but it does not remove the load. It also builds unity and gives momentum to the progress of the church as a whole. But the fact of the matter is constant effort must be maintained to keep congregants engaged in the process and doing their part.

Leaders will have to remind the membership of the character traits of perseverance and endurance found in the Scripture. These collide with our world's preference for instant gratification. Members need to stay the course. After all, most things of value take time to reach fruition.

"WHAT ABOUT US?"

Very few in the church will come right out and say this, but I assure you, many of them are thinking it. The argument goes something like this: "This is our church. Why are we doing this for 'them,' while they may never come? We're already here; our efforts should focus on us instead."

At first, this simply sounds baldly selfish. And perhaps it is. At our sinful core, we all suffer from the desire to make ourselves the center of our universe. We want things our way, on our agenda, in our own good time. Of course, every person has needs and concerns that must be addressed, so the necessity of self-preservation is normal. But in the believer's life, the desire for control must be challenged.

God never calls you to do something He's not going to equip you to do.

God's Word calls on us to overcome selfishness through submission to the Holy Spirit. His presence in our lives will teach us to align our lives with His agenda. A part of that is God's love for all people and His desire for relationship with them, too. When God's people are obedient to His commands, they will live generous lives, putting others before themselves.

There is more to this matter, though. Such "selfish" statements may actually be a cry for help. When people are hurting inside, they may react like this, revealing a longing for deeper relationships with others. They need to experience the care and comfort of others, who will show the love of Jesus to them in real and tangible ways. They need to be reassured that they are valued and of importance, too.

These cries must not be ignored, for the church is responsible for making them become disciples, a process in and of itself. They must learn their role in God's worldwide drama through modeling, through experience, and through education. But as they grow, just as in the material world, they must learn to give themselves away. This is one of the greatest lessons in all of life.

There is another concern this statement reveals. It suggests a lack of faith in God to provide for their own needs, while being used of God to touch the needs of others. Such lack of faith may cause individuals or entire churches to withdraw from engagement with others, and rather seek to create a protective cocoon from the rest of the world. God, though, wants to demonstrate to us He can be trusted. The only way this can happen is for us to choose to lean on Him when we cannot provide for ourselves. It is a choice we must make.

My uncle, a minister himself in Arkansas, once told me, "God never calls you to do something He's not going to equip you to do." I believe my Uncle Johnny was right. If God has called the church to reach out to others, then He is not abandoning you. He is taking your concerns upon Himself, as you take up His concerns as your own (Matthew 6:23-34).

"WE DON'T REALLY CARE THAT MUCH"

Finally, I mention to you another obstacle you may encounter that can cancel your entire journey forward for God. And it is may be the most important and genuine concern you will encounter. Most churches just do not care about lost people very much. Certainly not enough.

Again, as I stated on the last concern, this is a statement you will not hear recited or written anywhere, but it is as real as the nose on your face. It is the real elephant in the room of most declining churches. Evangelism is not on their hearts or in their heads. It is not a part of their budgets or their calendar. And as a result, evangelistic prayer or planning are not a part of congregational life.

There may be many reasons for this. In my opinion, apathy and complacency are at the top of the list. Believers just do not seem to care for the lost as they should. They have lost their first love, and this has affected everything else they do (or don't do!). The culture of comfort has invaded our churches. Too many congregations fail to have a burden for the lost around them; they rarely think or concern themselves with the eternal destiny of these unredeemed souls. Churches live like "Christian atheists,"[76] and few take up the task of "erasing hell."[77]

This mitigates against the urgency of the moment, the life-and-death nature of the human soul. I was taught as a teenager that churches preach about heaven and hell in tough times, as it gives hope, comfort, and motivation for perseverance during those times. Conversely, when "things" are good for society and for the people in our churches, songs about eternity diminish. Members fail to see the need, and they are often unmotivated to seize the moment.

Every 3.6 seconds a soul dies and enters eternity without hope and without Jesus.[78] This means somewhere in the world, 313,111 people are dying every day, and a large portion of them are heading to an eternity in hell. Some of these souls live in our communities, within sight of our church facilities. Others are within reach of our outreach and missions efforts around the world. Yet, we do little or nothing in many churches. Does this bother us at all?

As a church, and as pastors and leaders, we must prioritize our responsibility to share the Good News with others. We must care about their eternal destiny to the degree that it moves us to action. This does not happen by accident.

Intentionalize this priority in the strategy planning of the church. Budget for it accordingly. Give events and opportunities an evangelistic element. Then, as faith commitments are realized in the church, celebrate these decisions. Disciple these new believers, and over time, this process—maybe even these individuals—will breathe new life into the church, and growth will once again be the norm.

#renewbook

Last year, at an event where Alan Hirsch was speaking he made the startling statement, "Your system is perfectly designed for the results you are getting."[79] Wow. If this statement is accurate, leaders must re-examine the programs, processes, and priorities of the church's life together. Begin with the end in mind. Then chart a course to return the church to greater nurture, growth, and outreach.

Churches, like individuals, have a purpose here on earth. My prayer is your church refuses to stop short of fulfilling all that *"God has planned in advance for [it] to do"* (Ephesians 2:10).

Keep your eyes on God, for He is your North Star.
Keep in step with the Spirit, for He is your Counselor.
Keep Jesus at the center of all you do, for He is your Lord.

APPLY TO YOUR SETTING

1. What excuses have kept us from revitalization and growth efforts in the past? Why?

2. Which of these excuses challenge our people most at this time? How will we confront it?

3. How will we champion endurance, perseverance, and hard work on the journey? What other temptations could cause us to give up, quit, or lose focus during our effort?

QUESTIONS TO CONSIDER

1. How concerned are we over the lostness of people around us?

2. Are we selfish in how we do church? How important is our own comfort to us?

3. Do we trust God to provide for all our needs?

4. What is the biggest obstacle we face in finishing the journey successfully?

DIGGING DEEPER

Chan, Francis & Sprinkle, Preston. **Erasing Hell.** Colorado Springs, CO: David C. Cook, 2011.

George, Carl F. and Logan, Robert E. **Leading & Managing Your Church.** Old Tappan, NJ: Fleming H. Revell Company, 1987.

Groeschel, Craig. **The Christian Atheist.** Grand Rapids, MI: Zondervan Publishing, 2011.

Hirsch, Alan and Ford, Lance. **Right Here Right Now.** Grand Rapids, MI: Baker Books, 2011.

Sweet, Leonard. **Carpe Mañana.** Grand Rapids, MI: Zondervan, 2001.

ReNEW:
Traveling the Forgotten Path

EPILOGUE

WHERE DO WE GO FROM HERE?

"If our church closed its doors tomorrow, would the community even know we were gone? Previously, I would have wondered whether or not others would have noticed," Pastor Stephen said, as he addressed the congregation on this commemorative Sunday morning. "But God has transformed us over the past three years; He has given us the grace and the vision to make a difference for others again.

"Today's worship experience exemplifies this reality for us, for I share the platform with our town's Mayor, the School Superintendent, our Mission Agency's representative for West Africa, and the regional Recovery Center. These friends and neighbors have blessed us with the privilege of serving them and the townspeople here...as well as those in need on the other side of the world. The love of Christ through you has made a difference.

"Among us today are new followers of Christ; you have brought joy and celebration to our church family! We celebrate you as we celebrate the Lord who gives new life. This is our congregational life calling from God. Now, you too are to take up this calling and be disciple-makers yourselves. Together, we can make a difference.

"Have you ever heard anyone say, 'Be patient with me; God's not through with me yet?' Well, that is certainly true of us here at First Church; God has shown us we have many more ways to serve our Lord as we continue our journey with Him. I stand before you today, convinced God still wants us to make a difference!"

Pastor Stephen finished as he said, "So, where do we go from here? Today I proclaim to you this: while the destination is unknown, our traveling companion is well-known! Wherever God takes us, that indeed is where we will go! Where He leads us, we will follow!"

What about your church? If it closed its doors tomorrow, would anyone notice? Would it matter to anyone? This is truly a haunting question, but in reality, one I believe God challenges all of us to ask. In truth, only eternity will reveal the genuine impact any church has had on earth, as well as in the age to come. Yet, it is my contention we should allow the Spirit of God to show us ways in which we can extend our impact for the Kingdom and make a difference in the lives of others.

We do this because Jesus calls us.
We do this because Jesus cares.
We do this because others depend on us to share.

I grew up in something of a Christian bubble in the deep South, here in the United States. This bubble insulated me from the reality that people around me didn't know about Jesus, or the Good News, for themselves. It was not until my college days, when I met someone from another part of my country, that I realized for the first time others did not even know who Jesus is, much less what He had done on their behalf.

If your church has forgotten this reality—or fails to live like it is true—I hope this book has brought conviction and determination to correct this. If it has been in decline or struggling to stay alive, I pray this book has opened your eyes to the possibilities of what God wants to do among and through you. It all starts with recognizing where you are, and at the same time, who He is. It continues with the journey of a lifetime, as He invites you to partner with Him in Kingdom efforts for all eternity!

It all starts with recognizing where you are, and at the same time, who He is.

#renewbook

In 2014 I served as the transitional pastor of Faith Baptist Church in Glen Burnie, Maryland. While I was there, I had the privilege of working with a fine staff of creative, capable leaders within the church. One of them, Rev. Dr. Clarence Byerly, presented me with a gift not long before my departure. It was a walking stick he had fashioned, designed, and polished, just for me. Apparently, Rev. Byerly has made many of these walking sticks for various individuals over the years; I am honored that he included me in this elite circle of special people he has touched in this way.

The walking stick means a lot to me, personally. It is obviously functional, and thus, is helpful to me on the hiking trails and journeys that are a part of my life. But symbolically, it is valuable, too. It represents the reality that church—really, all of life—is a journey, and we do well to be prepared to embrace it with the best tools and wisdom we can embrace.

I pray that this book is a "walking stick" for your church, a tool to help you on the journey God wants you to take. A journey of renewal, a journey of revitalization.

And if you have journeyed together with God in applying these truths within your church and can celebrate along with Pastor Stephen, then I also celebrate with you. Reaching the destination God has in mind is a tremendous achievement, worthy of rejoicing. No doubt, you have had some moments when you or others in the church have asked, "Are we there yet?!" In these moments, I hope you came to realize the journey itself is half the fun and worthy of celebrating, too. On the path, God teaches us many lessons that prepare us for the future, including that eventual destination. Do not miss these special experiences, for they become the stories we pass on to a new generation of travelers coming our way.

If you have indeed reached that destination, you have probably discovered something else, too. God brings you to a vista point, only to reveal to you the next stage in the journey. You could not see it from where you were previously; now that you have made it this far, He can show you more.

#renewbook

So, don't give up now!
The ReNEW-al has only begun.

Dream a new dream with God.
Boldly go where no one has gone before (you get the idea).
And may God lead you every step of the way.

NOTES

INTRODUCTION

[1] Pastor Joe was introduced in the previous book I wrote, entitled *PLANTED: Starting Well, Growing Strong*, Severn, MD: Screven and Allen Publishing, 2012, p. 1. His five-year journey in establishing his new church is elaborated there, at the beginning of each chapter. In a similar way, Pastor Stephen is introduced here, whose ministry overlaps that of Pastor Joe, in a multi-year journey toward revitalization of First Church, and is chronicled at the beginning of each chapter in this book.

[2] Thom & Joani Schultz, *Why Nobody Wants to Go to Church Anymore*, Loveland, CO: Group, 2013, pp. 14-27. See also James Emory White, *The Rise of the Nones*, Grand Rapids: Baker Books, 2014, pp. 13-18.

[3] Robert D. Dale, *To Dream Again*, Nashville: Broadman, 1981, pp. 33-87, focuses on the dream, beliefs, goals, and structure that lead churches to grow, calling such churches "healthy." David Miles, *Restoring Beauty to the Bride Resource Kit*, Anaheim, CA: Church Resource Ministries, 2004, version 1.2, indicates the same, p. 9.19.

[4] The thesis of *PLANTED: Starting Well, Growing Strong*, Severn, MD: Screven and Allen Publishing, 2012, is there are certain characteristics in church plants that make them more effective evangelistically than established churches. Applying these characteristics can positively impact any church, regardless of age. See page 9.

CHAPTER ONE

[5] Michelle Obama introduced the *Let's Move!* campaign on childhood obesity, February 9, 2010 from the created Task Force on Childhood Obesity, The White House, Washington, D.C.

[6] Keith Green, *"To Obey is Better than Sacrifice,"* written by Green, is found on his second album, entitled *"No Compromise,"* Sparrow Records, 1978, track ten.

[7] Amy Grant, *"Fat Baby,"* written by Steve Millikan and Rod Robison, is found on her sixth album, *"Age to Age,"* Myrrh Records, 1982, track five.

[8] *PLANTED: Starting Well, Growing Strong*, Severn, MD: Screven and Allen Publishing, 2012, chapter 6, *"The Power of Relationships,"* pp. 75-86.
[9] Ibid., chapter 4, *"Passion for Those without Jesus,"* pp. 51-62.
[10] Ibid., chapter 9, *"In the Community,"* pp. 113-123.
[11] Ibid., chapter 5, *"Creativity and Innovation,"* pp. 63-74.
[12] My D.Min. studies in Christian Leadership at Gordon-Conwell Theological Seminary drilled into me this question as one of the most important questions any of us ever ask.
[13] *PLANTED: Starting Well, Growing Strong*, Severn, MD: Screven and Allen Publishing, chapter 7, *"Kingdom Citizens,"* pp. 87-98.

CHAPTER TWO
[14] *PLANTED: Starting Well, Growing Strong*, Severn, MD: Screven and Allen Publishing, 2012, chapter 2, *"Calling and Motivation,"* pp. 27-38.
[15] Ibid., chapter 3, *"Vision and Focus,"* pp. 39-50.
[16] Ibid., chapter 10, *"Limited Structure,"* pp. 125-136.
[17] Ibid., chapter 8, *"Budget and Time Priorities,"* pp. 99-111.
[18] Ibid., chapter 1, *"An Inspiring Leader,"* pp. 13-25.
[19] This online Facebook conversation took place in 2013 on my homepage, as we discussed the differences between church plants and established churches in the ability to influence them through pastoral leadership.
[20] In 2013, the Baptist Convention of Maryland/Delaware named "courage in leadership" to be one of the most crucial characteristics necessary for revitalizing churches effectively. This took place during their initial *Turning Around Journey* cohort, facilitated by Randy Millwood and me.

CHAPTER THREE
[21] William Shakespeare, *"The Tragedy of Richard the Third,"* Act 1, Scene 1, first line. *The Norton Facsimile: The First Folio of Shakespeare.* Prepared by Charlton Hinman. New York: W.W. Norton & Company, Inc., 1968, p. 527.
[22] John P. Kotter, *Leading Change*, Boston: Harvard Business Review Press, 2012, p. 46, in which "a sense of urgency" is the first

in his eight-stage process for leading change. This process was first published in 1996.

[23] Charles Duhigg, *The Power of Habit*, New York: Random House, 2012, pp. 1-30 *"The Habit Loop."*

[24] Tom Cheyney, *The Church Revitalizer as Change Agent*, Orlando, FL: Renovate Publishing Group, 2016.

[25] Holmes and Rahe Stress Scale, https://www.mindtools.com/pages/article/newTCS_82.htm.

[26] George Barna introduced this concept to me in his book by the same title, *The Frog in the Kettle*, Ventura, CA: Regal Books, 1990.

[27] Gary L. McIntosh and Charles Arn, *What Every Pastor Should Know*, Grand Rapids: Baker Books, 2013, pp. 173-176. Lyle E. Schaller, *Survival Tactics in the Parish*, Nashville: Abingdon Press, 1977, p. 27, is usually credited with this insight.

[28] John P. Kotter, *Leading Change*, Boston: Harvard Business Review Press, 2012, pp. 53-68, where he calls this group "the guiding coalition."

[29] Everett M. Rogers, *Diffusion of Innovations*, fifth edition. New York: Free Press, 1962, 2003, p. 281, charts out "Adopter Categorization on the Basis of Innovativeness," basically meaning how people respond to change. According to Rogers, when 16% are onboard, the majority will eventually follow. This has been revisited in recent years by Malcolm Gladwell, *The Tipping Point*, New York: Back Bay Books, Little, Brown and Company, 2012, 2013, with the rules of the Tipping Point (approximately the same percentage) impacted by The Law of the Few, the Stickiness Factor, and the Power of Context.

[30] *PLANTED: Starting Well, Growing Strong*, Severn, MD: Screven and Allen Publishing, 2012, chapter 10, *"Limited Structure,"* pp. 125-136.

CHAPTER FOUR

[31] Kenneth Quick, *Body Aches*, Carol Stream, IL: ChurchSmart Resources, 2009, pp. 13-29.

[32] The Annual Church Profile (ACP) is a data-keeping process for all Southern Baptist Convention (SBC) churches in North America. It charts all major numerical categories since 1960, if churches have been in existence that long. Check with the state convention office in

your area, if you are interested in learning how to access this information.

[33] Robert Dale, *To Dream Again*, Nashville: Broadman Press, 1981, p. 14, though he cites his insights come from the "provolutionary" model originally developed by Management Designs, Inc., of Cincinnati, OH, for the United Church of Christ.

[34] Mark Hallock, *God's Not Done with Your Church*, Littleton, CO: Acoma Press, 2017, and other related books in the RePlant series, specifically speak to the RePlant process for dying churches.

[35] Terry B. Walling, ReFocusing Network System is a two-stage process, using the *Focused Leaders* material in year one, and *Focused Living* material for the congregation in year two. Both are from Carol Spring, IL: SmartChurch Resources, 1998, 1996.

[36] Jim Collins, *Good to Great*, New York: HarperBusiness, 2001.

[37] Jim Collins, *How the Mighty Fall*, New York: HarperCollins Publishers, 2009, p. 20.

[38] *PLANTED: Starting Well, Growing Strong*, Severn, MD: Screven and Allen Publishing, 2012, chapter 3, pp. 39-50.

CHAPTER FIVE

[39] Kenneth Quick, *Healing the Heart of Your Church*, Carol Stream, IL: ChurchSmart Resources, 2003, pp. 83-148, dealing with issues like church splits, pastors who abuse, churches who abuse pastors, sinful reactivity, and shame.

[40] Ibid., chapters six through eight, pp. 57-80.

[41] *PLANTED: Starting Well, Growing Strong*, Severn, MD: Screven and Allen Publishing, 2012, p. 126, where I say, "Too much structure has the ability to stifle growth and development for any church, especially in the early days of its existence."

[42] Robert Dale, *To Dream Again*, Nashville: Broadman Press, 1981, chapter seven, pp. 88-102, on "The Promise and Threat of Ministry," for the church at the summit of the growth cycle is a must read. Note the top of page 96, especially.

CHAPTER SIX

[43] *PLANTED: Starting Well, Growing Strong*, Severn, MD: Screven and Allen Publishing, 2012, chapter one, pp. 13-25, dealing with your personal role in leadership.

[44] Charles R. Ridley and Robert E. Logan with Helena Gerstenberg, *Training for Selection Interviewing*, Carol Stream, IL: ChurchSmart Resources, 1998, Appendix A lists the Church Planter Performance Profile (CPPP), pp. 108-112.

[45] My D.Min. project focused on the Calling of Church Planters and developed a tool for use in discerning their calling. The tool is useful and can be obtained at no cost by contacting me through social media. See the author's page for details.

[46] Henry T. Blackaby and Claude V. King, *Experiencing God*, Nashville: Broadman & Holman Pubishers, 1994, pp.133-145.

[47] *PLANTED: Starting Well, Growing Strong*, Severn, MD: Screven and Allen Publishing, 2012, p. 17f.

[48] Gary L. McIntosh and Charles Arn, *What Every Pastor Should Know*, Grand Rapids: Baker Books, 2013, pp. 173-176. Lyle E. Schaller, *Survival Tactics in the Parish*, Nashville: Abingdon Press, 1977, p. 27, is usually credited with this insight.

CHAPTER SEVEN

[49] Daniel B. Wallace, *Greek Grammar Beyond the Basics*, Grand Rapids: Zondervan, 1997, p. 640, argues this is an attendant circumstance participle "used to communicate an action that, in some sense, is coordinate with the finite verb."

[50] Literally, this *hapax legonemon* ("one-time word" in the Bible) means "disciple" in verbal imperative form, like saying "disciple them!" He also notes that this includes baptizing them and teaching them to obey all Christ commanded, two other actions that indicate time must pass, and a process must take place.

[51] John Piper, *Let the Nations Be Glad*, Grand Rapids: Baker Books, 1993, p. 11.

[52] Brad Brisco, who currently serves as the Director of Bivocational Church Planting for the North American Mission Board, posted this on his Facebook page on October 17, 2017: "Our ecclesiology should flow out of mission, not the other way around. Mission is the mother of adaptive ecclesiology; meaning if we start with engaging in God's mission there should be lots of wild and wonderful expressions of church. The church DOES what it IS & then ORGANIZES what it DOES." (capitals from Brisco)

[53] Elmer Towns, Ed Stetzer, and Warren Bird, *11 Innovations in the Local Church*, Ventura, CA: Regal, 2007, p. 34. Ed Stetzer cites Alan Hirsch in his chapter *"Organic House Churches,"* on this.
[54] *PLANTED: Starting Well, Growing Strong*, Severn, MD: Screven and Allen Publishing, 2012, page 103.
[55] Gary L. McIntosh and Charles Arn, *What Every Pastor Should Know*, Grand Rapids: Baker Books, 2013, pp. 201-203.
[56] Thom Rainer, thomrainer.com, *"Five Problems with Church Programs,"* November 9, 2015.
[57] The Cooperative Program, a jointly-funded ministry stream for resourcing missions and ministry in the Southern Baptist Convention, was named in 1925, but likely would be called "a process" in today's language.
[58] Gary L. McIntosh and Charles Arn, *What Every Pastor Should Know*, Grand Rapids: Baker Books, 2013, pp. 163.
[59] Gary L. McIntosh, *Staff Your Church for Growth*, Grand Rapids: Baker Books, 2000, pp. 19-34.

CHAPTER EIGHT
[60] *PLANTED: Starting Well, Growing Strong*, Severn, MD: Screven and Allen Publishing, 2012, chapter six, pp. 75-86.
[61] James F. Engel and H. Wilbert Norton, *What's Gone Wrong with the Harvest?*, Grand Rapids: Zondervan, 1975. The well-known Engel Scale is shown on page 45.
[62] Larry Gilbert, Church Growth Institute, Lynchburg, VA, talked about this in his "TEAM Mate" tool, a part of TEAM Evangelism materials some years ago. It is still available for purchase at churchgrowth.org; the tool outlines a "stair step" strategy to personalize evangelism and analyze whether individual people are moving closer to Christ, in a way similar to the Engel scale, while at the same time, acknowledging it typically takes between seven and twenty-two "touches" today before someone commits their live to following Christ.
[63] W. Oscar Thompson, Jr. with Carolyn Thompson, *Concentric Circles of Concern*, Nashville: Broadman Press, 1981, pp. 13-27.
[64] Abby Stocker, *"The Craziest Statistic You'll Read about North American Missions,"* *Christianity Today* magazine, August 19,

2013, cites a study done at Gordon-Conwell's Center for the Study of Global Christianity, *"Christianity in Its Global Context, 1970-2000,"* saying that 20 percent of non-Christians (13.4 million people) in North America do not "personally know" any Christians.

[65] Marshall Shelley, *Ministering to Problem People in Your Church*, Bloomington, MN: Bethany House Publishers, 1985, 2013, pp. 41-58, lists several "well intentioned dragons" you may encounter in church life.

[66] *PLANTED: Starting Well, Growing Strong*, Severn, MD: Screven and Allen Publishing, 2012, chapter nine, pp. 113-123.

CHAPTER NINE

[67] Stephen R. Covey, *The 7 Habits of Highly Effective People*, New York: Fireside Books, 1989, *Habit Two: Begin with the End in Mind,* p. 95.

[68] John Maxwell, One Day Conference on Raising Up Leaders, Gordon-Conwell Theological Seminary, South Hamilton, MA, ca. 1999.

[69] J.D. Greear, *Gaining by Losing*, Grand Rapids: Zondervan, 2015, makes an excellent case for why established churches should do this.

CHAPTER TEN

[70] Mark Buchanan, *The Rest of God*, Nashville: Thomas Nelson, 2006. The theology of rest is not seen often, but is highly needed in the Western world.

[71] Aubrey Malphurs, *Advanced Strategic Planning*, 3rd edition. Grand Rapids: Baker Books, 2013, is a great resource for working through this process.

[72] Edward Mote, ca. 1834; William B. Bradbury, 1863. Hymn based on Matthew 7:24-27.

CHAPTER ELEVEN

[73] *"Snowmeggedon name traced back to CWG (Capital Weather Gang),"* The Washington Post, February 19, 2010, for the storm that came February 4-6 and dumped 18-32 inches of snow across the region.

[74] Carl F. George and Robert E. Logan, *Leading and Managing Your Church*, Old Tappan, NJ: Fleming H. Revell Company, 1987, called these people "formerberries" and "newberries." Chapter 10 is all about the Berry Bucket Theory, which speaks to this issue, and is well worth your attention, pp. 147-164.

[75] *Pareto's Principle* is a principle named after economist Vilfredo Pareto, that specifies an unequal relationship between inputs and outputs. The principle states that 20% of the invested input is responsible for 80% of the results obtained." (Investopedia.com) This principle, also known as the 80/20 Rule, has been extended, generally speaking, into all areas of life, including church life, stating 20% input is responsible for 80% of the results.

[76] Craig Groeschel, *The Christian Atheist*, Grand Rapids: Zondervan, 2010.

[77] Francis Chan and Preston Sprinkle, *Erasing Hell*, Colorado Springs, CO: David Cook, 2011.

[78] Steward, David J. *"Billions of People are Going to Hell."* jesus-is-savior.com, March, 2016.

[79] Alan Hirsch, Church Planting Leadership Fellowship, Nashville, TN, November, 2015.

ABOUT THE AUTHOR

James David Jackson (he prefers to be called David) grew up in the Bible Belt of America as a preacher's kid (PK) during the Civil Rights movement and the Cold War. He lived in Alabama, Tennessee, Texas, and Louisiana before graduating, and heading off to college in Arkansas. Earning his bachelor's degree from Ouachita Baptist University (a third consecutive generation graduate of the school), he earned his Master of Divinity degree from Southwestern Baptist Theological Seminary in Fort Worth, Texas. He went on to earn additional degrees from Princeton Theological Seminary (Th.M.) and Gordon-Conwell Theological Seminary (D.Min.), as well as doing further studies at Fuller Theological Seminary and Southern Baptist Theological Seminary.

He currently serves as the Church Planting Director/Strategist for the Baptist Convention of New England (an appointed position of the North American Mission Board). He has previously served in the same position with the Baptist Convention of Maryland/Delaware, and as the New Work Strategist for the Greater Boston Baptist Association.

Jackson has pastored churches in Arkansas and Massachusetts, in addition to service in revitalizing churches in California, Maine, and Maryland (some of them pastorates, and some intentional transitional interim pastorates). He has planted churches in New Hampshire and Massachusetts, as well. The combination of these experiences has enabled Jackson to recognize, implement, and experience the juxtaposition of church planting principles in revitalization situations.

He is happily married to his lovely wife Joyce since 1985. They have three amazing grown children: Sarah in New York City, Jonathan in up-state Georgia, and Rebekah here in Massachusetts. He has written two previous books, *PlantLIFE: Principles and Practices in Church Planting* (2008) and *PLANTED: Starting Well, Growing Strong* (2012). He is an avid Red Sox and Patriots fan and travels the nooks and crannies of New England with regularity.

He can be found online
at facebook.com/jdavidjacksonwriter,
at instagram.com/jdavid_jackson, and
at twitter.com/jdavid_jackson.

He welcomes your comments, critiques, and questions at any of the above locations.

~ 191 ~

www.ingramcontent.com/pod-product-compliance
Lightning Source LLC
Chambersburg PA
CBHW070604100426
42744CB00006B/402